Ethics by Design:

Strategic Thinking and Planning for Exemplary Performance, Responsible Results, and Societal Accountability

Stephanie L. Moore, Ph.D.

HRD Press, Inc. • Amherst • Massachusetts

Published by: HRD Press, Inc.
22 Amherst Road
Amherst, MA 01002
800-822-2801 (U.S. and Canada)
413-253-3488
413-253-3490 (fax)
www.hrdpress.com

ISBN 978-1-59996-201-6

Production services by Jean Miller
Editorial services by Sally Farnham
Cover design by Stephanie L. Moore

Table of Contents

For Justin

Foreword

In this important book, Dr. Moore accurately points out that ethics are both sensible and are at the core of any continuingly successful organization. She defines ethics both pragmatically and theoretically, gives cases-in-point, and provides tools and guidance to assure that you and your organization will harvest the positive results of thinking ethically and acting ethically. She also gives examples of organizations that only provided lip service to ethics and the consequences of doing so. The book gives essential guidance for those who would follow Peter Drucker's sage advice: It is more important to do what is right than it is to do things right. Ethics is about doing what is right.

It takes her only four succinct chapters to make the case: The Social Contract, Socially Desirable Ends, Nailing Mud: Socially Responsible Strategic Planning, and Defining Excellence: Ethics in Performance Standards.

With many hands-on exercises and multiple examples, this book provides you with the tools and concepts to make you and your organization successful. And continue to be successful.

One can run from being ethical but ultimately cannot hide from it. Hiding is not a responsible option. What is foolish and self-destructive is foolish and self-destructive.

And so it is with the topic of ethics. Excuses will lead to failure and liability. Following the solid material here will allow you to be successful.

And practical. And Ethical by Design.

Roger Kaufman, Ph.D., CPT
Distinguished Research Professor,
Sonora (Mexico) Institute of Technology
Professor Emeritus, Florida State University

Preface

Prior to 2008, most especially the summer and fall economic fallouts, the case made in this book might have been a bit harder sell. While there is plenty of evidence behind the models and arguments put forward in this book, by and large most folks—especially the leadership of the U.S.—were content to roll along according to the old model and old mind-sets.

Now we see that the old model failed us—in a large, interconnected manner.

As one of the few to step forward and take responsibility for the failings, Alan Greenspan captured this succinctly:

> "Yes, I found a flaw in the model that I perceived is the critical functioning structure that defines how the world works ..."[1]

Indeed, we all together found the flaw, or rather, are experiencing the consequences of the flaw. But when the facts change, so should your mind change.

But the flaw doesn't reside with a single individual or a single firm or organization, although the decisions and actions of individuals and organizations led to the widespread failures.

> "The crash of the stock market and the crash of Bernie Madoff together are really emblematic that the system is the culprit." – Alexandra Penney[2]

Yes—the system is the culprit, or rather, one's view of "the system" and how that system is designed is the culprit. Greenspan's "system" design had limitations—limitations that are addressed when we adopt a more robust definition of "system" and plan or design for desired results in the larger system.

In this book I provide the concepts, ideas, and tools to keep you and others from designing and delivering a disaster plan. And it all centers on ethics.

Probably no topic is quite so slippery to get our arms around as ethics, and yet there are few other topics that more pervade all our lives, that we all think about in some form.

Although a philosopher will quickly think of Kierkegaard or Sartre or Plato, others who have never read those pieces will have equally strong opinions and ideas on ethics as well. Often, when I bring up ethics in conversation, others jump to talking about individuals and ethics—what this person or that person did in the office, or what some company did that costs thousands their pensions. While individuals play an obvious role in ethical decisions, the focus here is really on **system ethics** and what that implies for effective strategic planning, accountability, and performance design. The design of the system greatly influences decisions, behaviors, performance and results. We have discovered that more of human behavior is influenced by the eco-system around people.[3] We design flaws and frailties into our systems—into laws, policies, incentives, unintentional disincentives, physical infrastructures, educational practices, technologies, information. Whether we are conscious of it or not, we create gaps, and we individually and organizationally pay the price for these flaws to continue to exist. Conversely, we can design our strengths and our insights into these systems—if we so choose. This book is for those of you who choose to design a different system—a future you want your children to inhabit, that you wish you could live long enough to experience.

"Ethics by design" is the notion that we are participants in a larger whole—the larger system of society; it is an acknowledgment that decisions have results and that we accomplish those desired results through a deliberate effort to plan and design towards desirable results. Desirable is defined at the societal level—not the individual or the organizational. And this isn't utilitarianism. It's not about the greatest good for the greatest number. Majority or minority have no place here. Instead, it is total and holistic—*system ethics*—everything is inter-related. A product here or a service there or a new technology has ripple effects. "Unintended consequences" is no longer an acceptable argument—for in many cases, we've passed a tipping point for the collective "unintended consequences" of many organizations and entities, all adding up to one larger societal failure. Whether it is mass genocides, environmental damage, terrorism, unconscionable financial activities, drastic economic fallouts, or spread of serious disease—none of these are possible without system-wide failures.

Ethics by design means we begin at the top level and, with stakeholders, design ethics into everything we do, starting with what we deliver to society linking that on down into our organization and the individuals within the organization. It's not about foregoing profits (or ratings or funding) but rather about ensuring long-term viability (including economic viability) by way of continually delivering results that are of benefit to society and to the stakeholders (not just stockholders) in the system. Desirable, ethical performance from organizations won't start until it becomes a part of accountability models—what the desired impact of an organization and its products or services should be, and how you are planning for desired impact on society. Desirable, ethical behavior won't start in employees unless it becomes a systemic feature of your organization—how the "eco-system" of your organization is designed to support desirable performance and how desired impact of your organization is aligned down into tasks, processes and inputs.

If you are ready to be a part of a better system design—and better results—then this book is for you. What is detailed in here is both a model for planning for desirable social results as well as a new definition of accountability—one that focuses on societal impact and results rather than just the more conventional internal processes and isolated individual performance results. Societal impact is about doing the right things; internal processes are about doing things right. Many organizations have done things right (i.e. have well-established processes) without doing the right things (i.e., yield undesirable results)—that is the flaw. When you and your organization focus on doing the right things, then align your processes to do things right, the end result will be one we all can live with.

Endnotes

1. NPR story, Oct. 23, 2008; *Greenspan: U.S. Will Take Months to Recover.*

2. Contributor, TheDailyBeast.com and investor in Madoff, CNN Money, Jan. 12, 2009 by Christine Romans (http://money.cnn.com/video/#/video/news/2009/01/12/news.mad offvictim-010908.cnnmoney).

3. See *Performance by Design* by Watkins, 2007; Deming, 1972, 1982, 1986; Juran, 1988.

Chapter 1
The Social Contract

"All of this could have been avoided had the company not put profit ahead of safety."

Reporter commentary on recall of defective tires for SUVs, 2007[1]

"Safety is everybody's responsibility. It's not just the federal government's job to catch safety defects."

Olivia Alair, spokeswoman for the National Highway Traffic Safety Administration, commenting on 2010 Toyota recalls[2]

As Real As It Gets

The consequences for lack of ethical standards integrated into decision making processes are staggering, and they have hit every single one of us already. Whether you have lost a loved one to defective products, lost your health due to poor environmental practices, lost your retirement after stock in a company or a financial institution went belly up and the CEO went to jail, lost your house as a result of unsafe banking practices, or even lost potential earnings because of discriminatory practices, you have experienced the very real consequences of systemic unethical behavior.

We *can* measure the impact of lack of ethics—in perhaps the most real terms possible. We can measure it in terms of lives lost, permanent physical injury, deleterious health infractions, gender or age or race disparity across organizations resulting in differential survival and quality of life, disabling illnesses, poverty, crime rates, self-sufficiency, terminal environmental damage, and even war, terrorism, and riot (in Chapter 2, we will look at a framework for these measurements). In essence, we can measure and know whether our actions and products have been socially responsible.

Estimates on costs of unethical behavior put the price tag at $3 trillion dollars a year—*just* in the United States, and *just* in the for-profit sector.[3] Thus, that figure does not include costs in government, non-profit, military and education sectors, or any estimates from international entities. These figures also reflect only acts like embezzlement and theft, but do not include any estimated costs for settlements over deaths, injuries, discrimination, environmental impact or other measures of social irresponsibility. The costs and consequences of the absence of ethics in organizations and organizational planning are indeed staggering—both to the organization and to society.

By contrast, the benefits of ethics integrated into organizational performance—at all levels—amount to some "holy grails" of success that many organizations strive for but few achieve. Businesses that deliver desirable results to society, and products that have a desirable impact, enjoy long-term success and profit over many years, not just short-term successes. These same businesses attract top talent and employees who want to work in an ethical setting that makes meaningful contributions, thereby allowing the organization to maintain a workforce that is inherently driven by ethics as part of their practice and remains loyal to the organization over many years. Turnover decreases, productivity increases, and profits increase—and society wants that organization to keep delivering the same or more. Organizations which possess, apply, and communicate strong ethical core values—such as stakeholder service, social responsibility, ethics, and sustainability[4]—are just as, if not more, financially successful than their corporate counterparts.[5]

When these benefits are understood, there really is no better business plan[6] than one that integrates ethics from the get-go.

A strengthening trend across professions over the past 50 years has led to more fields like law, business, medicine and engineering integrating ethics into their professional training and higher education curricula, recognizing that ethics are an important part of professional practices and a desired characteristic of the new workforce.[7] Some of these professions have been forced—by society—to do so after patterns of practice led society to conclude the profession was not willing or able to regulate itself. After the Watergate scandal, for example, law schools were required to provide a course on legal ethics that every student now has to take.

However, just because ethics are part of a curriculum or published guidelines does not mean they are part of standard business practices or on-the-job performance once employees hit the field. Recent studies indicate that fully one-third to one-half of all employees have observed unethical activities, and on average only half of all employees say they would report unethical activities to management (ERC, 2005; HR Focus, 2006).

Of even more concern is the lack of ethics integrated into decision-making processes, organizational planning and management models. Not only does lack of ethics at the top lead to apathy among employees, which yields the results in the studies cited above, but it leads to major organizational and societal failures. The economic fallout of 2008 and Sarbanes-Oxley are among some of the most notable evidence of this. In the past decade, a string of corporate scandals with irregular accounting practices led to failed or weakened companies, cost thousands of US citizens their pensions and jobs, and destabilized the US economy by causing downturns in the stock market and frightening investors. Companies like Enron, WorldCom, Madoff, Fannie Mae, Freddie Mac, and Tyco have become the face of widespread ethical failures.[8] The massive economic fallout in the financial sector in fall of 2008 that required government bailouts is the direct result of companies planning for short-term profits, using tactics that in the long run have dire societal impact, while being facilitated by well-meaning but short-sighted legislation. As the rebuilding of that sector takes shape, a focus on how a rebuilding and design of that sector could actually lift the local and global economy would be the only way to accurately reflect just how interwoven the organizations are with the fabric of society (see the "Stakeholders ≠ Stockholders" sidebar).

Stakeholders ≠ Stockholders or Shareholders

"'Yes, I found a flow in the model that I perceived is the critical functioning structure that defines how the world works, so to speak. . . .I was shocked because I had been going for 40 years or more with very considerable evidence it was working exceptionally well.'

"The flaw, he believed, was his view that financial institutions can be relied upon to operate in their own self-interest. That, he thought, would provide sufficient protection for shareholders. . ." (NPR story, Oct. 23, 2008; Greenspan: U.S. Will take Months to Recover)

Nothing highlights the difference between stakeholders and stockholders (or shareholders) more than this flaw in the model that has driven the U.S. economy for a long time. Organizations that plan for benefits to shareholders are still planning internally—the true stakeholders are all of society, regardless of who actually purchases stock in a given company or institution. A focus on letting institutions operate in their own self-interest is still a very "internal" definition of organizational planning—that organizations are entities unto themselves that will do no harm to others external to them, so long as they plan well internally and "succeed" in terms of profit that they generate.

The flaw is highlighted by systemic thinking and systemic ethics—all organizations are parts of a larger system, and their planning must include planning that addresses what they deliver to the larger system of society—stakeholders—not just what they deliver to those internal to a given organization—stockholders. To take this even further, it is not enough to include societal-level planning in organizational planning, but in fact organizations have to start with societal-level

(continued)

Stakeholders ≠ Stockholders or Shareholders (concluded)

> **planning to align desired societal impact down into what they do, produce, and deliver.**
>
> **Because of the systemic, interrelated nature of the world, every individual in society is a stakeholder in what organizations do, produce, and deliver. Whether we buy an organization's products, services, or stock in those companies—or not—we are impacted by how they do business.**
>
> **If the lack of systemic planning at the societal/system-level was the flaw—what Hugh Oakley-Browne calls "the collapse of the USA 'ONE BOTTOM LINE' model" (personal communications, 2008)—then efforts for going forward have to include societal-level, systemic planning as the core characteristic.**

Furthermore, companies that plan for positive social impact actually wind up staying in business far longer and being more profitable.[9] Leaders of these companies are excellent at detailing a vision focused on the desired social conditions that should exist for their companies to be successful, and then shaping their companies' mission statements that then align downward into the companies' products, processes, and inputs.[10] Conversely, organizations that ignore the surrounding conditions of their ventures can run blind to circumstances that will impede growth and success. Citing analyses of foreign markets in India, China, the Middle and Far East, Latin America and Africa, Bernárdez explains,

> "those companies that enter emerging markets driven exclusively by maximizing short-term financial and cost-efficiency goals without defining a social value-added strategy may in fact be taking much higher risks in the form of market stagnation, legal insecurity, riots, damage to property and lives, and business disruption

than those that link those bottom line results to proactive social value-added and improvement goals."[11]

Ethics simply start at the top—not as a code of ethics or a code of conduct, which often become window dressing—but as an actual strategic-related business plan. Ethics are a means for defining exemplary performance and exemplary deliverables (both consequences and products)—not just for individuals, but for organizations of all types. Indeed, ethical performance *is* exemplary performance. Anything short of this is not sustainable excellence.

Not only does the external context impact organizations, but your organization impacts the external context. Without ethics in decision making processes, people die, food is contaminated, poverty increases, crime increases, and populations that are discriminated against face deepening inequity. These are not indicators of exemplary performance. These are failures that we design into systems—consciously or unconsciously. When these failures occur, an organization (be it corporate or government or public or some other configuration) or an entire profession (like education or engineering or law or medicine) breaks a social contract with society—and society lets the organization or profession know they don't like it. The "marketplace" isn't just some segment of the population, a vague nameless, faceless entity. The "marketplace" is our shared and interdependent society—the ultimate system, into which we infuse our products and services, and into which we graduate professionals of various disciplines. Every organization and profession, of any type, has an impact on society that, when planned and managed effectively, leads to great benefits for everyone... and when handled poorly leads to undesirable results. This is what Roger Kaufman calls *Mega Planning*[12] and what Ian Davis calls "the biggest contract"[13]—and when a plane crashes, or parts malfunction, or our service leads to a social divide, society calls us on our contractual obligations.

In short, ethics by design is about planning for desirable consequences or managing the biggest contract. Whether it's the consequences of what the engineers in your company design and manufacture, or the consequences of your business model on the local (or global) economy, or the consequences of graduates from your school who do or do not have certain skills and knowledge, your organization yields societal consequences. Those consequences are accomplished by choice—by design (and neglect is a form of choice). So, in this book, we'll look at how to lasso a typically messy topic into an effective form of strategic planning, focused on a number of societal consequences.

Before we go any further, it should be noted that this book addresses all types of organizations—business, education, government, non-profit and even military. Every single one of these types of organizations is a smaller subsystem within the larger system of society. What you do, produce, and deliver in each one of those impacts society—and on an increasingly global scale. Your organization has a contract with society. While social responsibility has tended to focus on private, for-profit organizations, the truth is that all our organizations contribute different results to society. Education, health, government and non-profit sectors are facing similar scrutiny over perceived failures to deliver to society what these industries should. Ethical breakdowns in professional practice usually lead to heavy external regulation—so the increasing regulation not just in business but in education, health and government is the strongest indicator that contracts with society have not been well-managed.

So, if you are a leader (or intend to become one) in a for-profit or non-profit, an administrator in a local school district, part of a university's leadership or governance, a state governor or state secretary or administrator of a state agency or office, or even a military planner or strategist, this book is essential to what you do. You are at the helm of the outcomes your organization delivers to society (not just the products you make or outputs you deliver). For the many people in the middle, this is a path for integrating ethics in your departments or units, into your practices and processes to ensure that what you and your team send up the chain is adding value. This is the recipe for how your staff feels like their every-day tasks add up to something "meaningful" or "purposeful." For the individual, this is a way for you to determine if the organization you're working for (or the politician or ballot initiative you vote for, or the places you do business) really is an ethical, socially responsible organization—and if not, how to identify the places you want to work for or buy products from. And if you are a teacher or a college professor who develops tomorrow's planners, leaders, and employees, this content is a necessary part of your curriculum as you integrate ethics into decision making processes. It's also a necessary part of what your department (or college or university) does to model ethics in your profession. We will look at examples across all types of organizations in this book.

Get the Facts: Not Knowing Is No Longer Acceptable

A colleague of mine—Professor Dale Brethower—signs all his e-mails:

"If you care, get the facts."[14]

If you care—if your organization claims to be a caring organization, or even assumes care because of the nature of your work (like education or non-profits)—then get the facts. If you are accomplishing what you say you are and having the desired impact you think you are, get the facts.

We often confuse the products[15] we deliver to society (e.g. an automobile or a graduate) with the impact and consequences of those products on society. Your organization may produce tires, for example, but the mere production (and sales) of tires is not a measure of impact. You deliver millions of tires to the market. However, if your tires are defective, leading to blowouts or tread separation under certain conditions, then the *results* of your product are undesirable—rollovers, damage to property, injury, and loss of lives. These are the most undesirable results a company can deliver—and yet very real (recall the quote that began this chapter). The news is filled daily with reports of these very sorts of results.

For a long time, as standard practice organizations have stopped their data collection at the point of measuring outputs—literally. "What did we put out there?" "How high were our sales/profits this quarter?" "How many parts did we produce this month?" "How many students did we graduate this year?" "How much in funds did we distribute to people left homeless from a natural disaster?"

Outputs have an impact, though—and truly strategic, ethical planning includes getting the facts on what the outcomes of those outputs are (and what to do when it's not desirable—which aligns downward into your organizational processes): what is the societal impact of a drug, of a new governmental policy, of a law, of a new technology, and so forth. It goes beyond the intentions of the organizational outputs to also track the societal (Mega) consequences. So you produce more tires—so what? What does that matter if the tires are separating or blowing out and leading to death or injury? So you graduate more business majors or engineers into the workforce—so what? What happens if those graduates actually cause lost jobs or damage the environment via their practices? Or conversely, what if your graduates go on to create job opportunities that lift a community, build businesses or infrastructures that have a positive impact on the local community and environment, or institute safe engineering practices that lead to a decrease in structural failures, which in turn saves lives during natural disasters?

We can no longer assume that what we do, produce and deliver through our organizations is of benefit to the individuals served by our organization and to society at large. We may want them to benefit, or assume they do, but without data, we simply don't know and therefore can't plan towards desired impact. What we can assume is that our outputs have an impact on those individuals and society—but the assumption of a positive impact is a dangerous assumption. Your organization cannot assume it doesn't have a negative impact on the environment or suicide rates, for example (see Case Study below—Suicide Rates Among Returning Soldiers). High-stress environments, like air traffic control centers, can lead to higher rates of suicide or depression among employees. Ignoring these potential facts can blindside a company or organization and bring it down or put it out of business. Leaders have lost their jobs and entire careers due to this lack of sight. If you care about the outcomes of your organization, get the facts—get the data that tells you whether you're accomplishing desirable results or not.

Case Study

Suicide Rates Among Returning Soldiers— No Excuses for Not Getting the Facts

In 2007, CBS Worldwide news reported that suicide rates among veterans was twice the rate of non-veterans. As a result, the Veteran's Affairs Committee held a hearing in Congress to listen to both sides—families who had lost loved ones to suicide and the department of Veterans Affairs.[16] The Department of Veterans Affairs did dispute the statistics from the CBS report.[17] However, the committee chairman, Bob Finer, scolded the DVA for not getting the facts. He argued that the DVA failed to foresee this mental health epidemic by not collecting nationwide data on suicides. "You don't track this stuff. You simply don't track it. You don't want to know about it."[18]

While an organization of any sort may not track social impact measures related to their line of work, society will. And often, when an organization doesn't track this sort of data internally and use it to revise their products and processes, the data will be tracked publicly as society's interest is piqued and the general public keeps tabs. At this point, an organization begins to lose permission to self-regulate and it loses confidence in the public's eye—which leads to decrease in business, heavy external regulation, change in leadership, or even closure of that organization.

With facts in hand, the DVA could have (a) foreseen a trend compared to the national average, then (b) developed a plan to cut the problem off, (c) set very clear targets for the results their agencies' plans would deliver, and (d) publicly demonstrated that they cared enough to get the facts and do something about it, which goes a long way in public relations. With this sort of data, they could measure the effectiveness of programs developed to address suicide rates among veterans and adjust as necessary, depending on whether an increase or decrease to suicide rates occurred over time. This sort of planning and forecasting based on data and focused on results would save lives.

Social Responsibility—A Practical Definition for Effective Planning

"Social responsibility" has become the new tagline for the "caring organization" (it has also somehow become erroneously synonymous with environmental practices or giving to charity). As a result, social responsibility has sounded more like a feel-good campaign rather than a measurable, strategic course of action.

A distinction is in order between "corporate social responsibility" as it has been communicated and practiced to date and this book's definition of "social responsibility." Social responsibility is a result of applied ethics—emphasis on *applied*. There have been some truly noble and valuable efforts as a part of corporate social responsibility, and the intent here is not to discredit that work. However, the prevailing conception and application of corporate social responsibility often actually results in a potential disservice both to organizations and to society at large. Corporate social responsibility has tended to focus primarily on getting companies to adopt policies on social responsibility and develop some activities related to sustainability and environmental reports, or doing community service. Additionally, social responsibility has been treated as something that is "in addition to" an organization's core business or purpose—an additional layer (which often translates into an additional task list and therefore an additional irritation), rather than an integral part of the organization's strategic planning process. As a result, as Davis explains, social responsibility is often too narrowly defined in many organizations—reflected in corporate social responsibility commonly being housed in public- or corporate-affairs departments.[19]

However, social responsibility is far more than a sales campaign, and more than environmentalism or sustainability. It is more than a philosophical disposition, and it is more than charitable donations. Social responsibility is a way of doing business—regardless of whether your line of business turns a profit or not—that demonstrates added-value to society. The truly socially responsible organization can demonstrate it adds value: it gets the facts of impacts and consequences. This is ethics by design; this is "doing ethics" on purpose.

Social responsibility is a way of gearing your organization towards desirable societal outcomes in a manner recognizing that what you do, produce and deliver has an impact on society. It is purposefully planning for adding value to society in specific, measurable forms.

Social responsibility that actually has an impact is a way of being a partner with society as a whole—and doing business in a manner such that society wants you to continue doing business. No wonder there is a positive correlation between the two bottom lines—the financial bottom line and the social bottom line.[20] Society has a vested interest in seeing your organization perform well—because it has a lot at stake, whether it wants to or not, if you do *not* perform well.[21]

There's a reason a company's stock falls when it announces recalls or one of its products repeatedly explodes in rear-end accidents. An organization's performance is also evaluated on socially significant measures. In fact, a business model driven purely by short-term profitability can lead to disasters that eventually drive, and have driven, companies out of business.

Case Study

The Real Consequences—Failure at the Societal Level Can Cost You Your Organization

On September 25, 2007, Topps Meat Company, LLC, recalled 331,582 pounds of ground beef for possible E. coli contamination. Four days later, on September 29, 2007, Topps voluntarily expanded that recall to 21.7 million pounds of ground beef. Six days later, on October 5, 2007, Topps announced they were closing their 67-year-old business for good. The total beef recalled had amounted to one full year's worth of processing and work. The company simply couldn't overcome that loss of production and revenue.

(continued)

Case Study (concluded)

> For the company, the actions to correct the sources of the problem came too late. The recall also came too late for consumers—much of the meat under the recall had already been consumed, and 30 people across 8 states had E. coli infections matching the strain found in Topps' ground beef.
>
> Although the exact cause of the problem has not yet been announced from the investigation by the United States Department of Agriculture (USDA), the problem simply stated is this: somewhere down the line, there was a breakdown in procedure or process that led to a defective product, and there was an absence of safeguards to catch the defect that led to a dangerous product being delivered to market. The social impact: 30 serious illnesses, 1 company down, and 87 jobs lost. In addition to the measurable impact of the illnesses is the measurable economic impact on the employees and local economy in Elizabeth, New Jersey.[22]
>
> Health (or disease) and safety are one of the measurable social impacts an organization can have. Although not every organization impacts health and safety directly, many do. From products that malfunction, like poor tires or out-of-date or out-of-specification airplane parts, to foods and beverages to pollution, nearly every organization has an impact on the health and safety of society at large.

For government, educational and non-profit organizations, this definition of social responsibility is no less applicable. For many of these agencies or organizations, the intended purpose may appear on the surface to be an obvious social good. However, many get lost in processes and lose sight of these outcomes, and they may operate in a manner that is actually detrimental to society and to the individuals served by the organizations, however unintentional that detriment may be.

Social responsibility is a very different organizational model—one that shifts your focus from doing things right to doing the right things. There are some ethical or professional models founded upon the notion of doing things right (c.f. National Education Association Code of Ethics[23]). However, it is possible to do things right and still not deliver the desired outcomes.

Organizations that focus on "doing things well" often get lost in process, because that statement is all about process. Organizations that focus on "doing the right things" don't get lost in processes, but instead focus on delivering desired results, and continually modify or refine processes to ensure they align towards desired results.

For example, the purpose and mission of public education in the United States may be to ensure that every child receives the best education possible to become self-sufficient to the greatest degree possible by adulthood. Schools may do things right all the time—they may hire "highly qualified" teachers, submit the reports required by law, administer tests, collect the data, report data, send teachers to on-going professional development, purchase evidence-based curricula, and so on. But crossing off those processes on a compliance-oriented checklist may not actually change classroom practices or yield the intended results. In the end, students who graduate but cannot read, compose coherent thoughts, critically evaluate diverse information sources, or do the necessary basic math for competitive jobs are at a serious economic disadvantage as adults—made only more serious by an increasingly global economy in which they compete with a larger pool. We're excellent at processes and can get those right, but still miss the point entirely—we can still not accomplish the right things. Conversely, I have seen schools go from among the lowest performing in their states to the highest performing because a strong leader used data to penetrate processes and focus the entire school on actual performance and progress towards desired results. These leaders got the facts then rearranged and adapted processes to align them with desired ends—they focused on doing the right things, not just doing things right.

Families affected by a large natural disaster rely on local, state and federal entities to operate effectively and get them out of harm's way or get food and shelter to them in a timely manner. Veterans rely on government agencies to keep their personal data safe so what financial stability they do have is not threatened by identity theft that wipes out their financial self-sufficiency for retirement. For all the assumed social bene-fit of these types of organizations, these organizations may often get lost in processes and lose sight of the outcomes they deliver to society. When those failures to deliver results occur, we hear about them in the evening news.

System Thinking—Adding Value to the Whole

Doing the right things is a very external focus, while doing things right is a very internal focus. Organizations get lost in processes (and fail to deliver results) when they lose sight of the world around them and their external clients, be those clients consumers, families, children, elders, or the country depending on you to keep it secure. To focus on doing the right things and even think in terms of measuring socially responsible behavior, we have to first understand why society—*not* our organizations—is the starting point for strategic planning.

The days of thinking of an organization or institution in isolation from all other institutions and from society are long past.[24] Many do still operate this way, but that's a business model that will be short-lived. A brief boom in profit or ratings does not mean a business or organization is functioning in a way that will sustain continued success. Even though the "short-term" forecasts and outlooks are the standard, common models for many organizations, they are by no means the most accurate or reliable. A company with a large profit one year may very well be out of existence the next year without truly strategic planning towards socially desirable results.

We have come to understand our world—in a variety of disciplines, from physics and the natural sciences to the social sciences—as interconnected and interrelated. A change or action in one place has ripple effects into other places. This is the *systemic* way of thinking. It should not be confused with *systematic,* which means to follow a clearly defined process. Instead, system thinking views the parts as part of a whole— what happens in one part affects other parts and, therefore, affects the whole.

An important distinction is in order. The absence of the "s" at the end of "system" is not a typo. Much of this stems from General System Theory originally articulated by von Bertalanffy.[25] General System Theory has become an important paradigm shift of the 20th and 21st centuries, wherein we moved from viewing things in isolation to understanding that there are multiple parts, and a change in one part impacts other parts. However, most application of General System Theory became system*s* theory, resulting in a "parts" approach rather than a "whole" approach. Models or processes identify parts or stay completely subsumed within their own part, failing to recognize the other parts at play. The "s" on system slipped in over time, but von Bertalanffy originally conceived of General System Theory as a focus on the whole. The two paradigmatic differences between "system" and "systems" are indeed worlds apart, not just an "s" apart: one moves from the whole to the parts. This is socially responsible planning—starting with the desired whole and identifying your part in that, then planning your organization's outputs and processes in such a manner as to deliver those desirable results. The other moves from parts to the whole. When planning moves from parts to the whole, the whole winds up being a reactive shape based on the actions and constellation of the parts.

System Approach

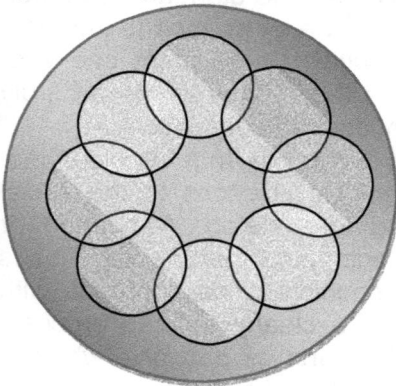

What do we want the whole to look like? What is my contribution or my organization's contribution to that whole?

Systems Approach

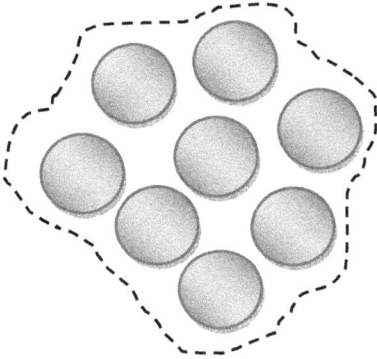

What are the parts and how do they relate? If we change this part, what other parts will we have to change as well?

Diffusion of innovations researcher Everett Rogers begins his explanation of change with the metaphor of marbles in a bowl.[26] Moving one marble in the bowl causes the other marbles to shift. That is an excellent line of research that has yielded valuable insights and tools for managing change. But new understandings about how the parts relate to the whole require a modification to this metaphor. For a long time, we have missed this impact of the movement of those parts on the larger whole. The bowl is apparently unaffected by all the change going on inside it. Typical "strategic" planning makes this same assumption—that the larger bowl is somehow unaffected by all the changes and shifts occurring within. While the metaphor is nice, in truth, the shape is greatly determined by the parts within. In reality, society is shaped by the subsystems, organizations, actions, and individuals within. The "bowl" doesn't come to us as a perfectly circular crystalline bowl with no blemishes off the factory line. It doesn't come to us at all—we shape it, continually. So not only are the parts within interconnected, but those parts add up to the shape of the whole. The system approach recognizes that the shape of that ultimate larger "bowl" holding us all is impacted by what's going on inside it; the shape of the bowl is impacted by the relationships and movements of the marbles. Systemic planning begins with the bowl—with the whole—rather than the parts. Desirable change takes the whole into consideration and starts there to align downward.

This is called "outside-in" planning,[27] which stands in stark contrast to conventional planning models. Many organizations plan internally for their organizational success without considering the external context. Organizations both impact this external context and are impacted by that context, so planning in a vacuum proves very short-sighted for any organization. In fact, organizations that begin with a vision for social impact and change are ones that *create* the ideal conditions for lasting success.[28] This is a much more proactive approach to change, where your organization defines the very sort of change it wants to create and be a part of, versus a reactive approach to change (which predominates many planning models and mindsets).

Ultimately, the "whole" is society—the collective "we" in our global society. What a business or organization does impacts society. When a food production company, such as Topps Meat, delivers a defective product to society, the impact ripples out to impact the people who get sick, their families, insurance rates, employees within the organization who lose their jobs and pension plans, their family members, and even the local economy. Everything is interrelated.

Ethics by design is the recognition that decisions add up to a larger whole—the larger system of society. Ethics have traditionally focused on individuals, but now the focus is on systemic implications. Desirable results are defined at the societal level, not just the organizational or the individual. This is not the same as utilitarianism. It's not about the greatest good for the greatest number. Majority or minority have no place here. Instead, it is *systemic ethics*—everything is inter-related. A product here or a service there or a new technology in that one has ripple effects.

When an airline operator doesn't inspect its fleet as often and comprehensively as it should, eventually a plane with faulty parts ends up in the sky with 300 passengers and their families praying for a good conclusion as they watch live coverage on the national news channels. When a government agency (or worse, a string of them) gets lost in processes and loses sight of real-world consequences, thousands of people end up homeless and without food or water in the face of a natural disaster, which in turn contributes to increased poverty and crime rates.

What a business or organization does, produces and delivers has an impact on the world—as a result, that interaction and interdependency calls for an updated way of thinking about how we plan and do business. We can no longer legitimately cease our planning where the walls of our office buildings end and the "world out there" begins. Planning—truly strategic planning—starts with society: what is the desired, measurable impact you and your organization will have on society. This is called "Mega" planning in the model derived by Kaufman.[29] Whether your organization is a for-profit corporation, educational institution, government agency (including the military), non-profit organization, or any other sort of organization—you ultimately deliver your products and services to society. That same society relies on you to do your business *well*.

In some of the examples cited above, the world of planning becomes incredibly complex. For example, when planning for natural disasters, planning looks like risk management—what are the most likely, least likely, and worst case scenarios. By no means will this book suggest a simplistic approach to such complex challenges. However, what I do suggest is that we are much better off in the long run—all of us, including your organization and the rest of us who depend on your organization or use your products or services—if we are conscious of the consequences of our decisions as we go through planning processes. The collective "we" of society will be safer, healthier, and more self-sufficient for it, and in return give you more of our trust and business which makes you more profitable (e.g. business products) or desirable (e.g., schools) and ensures your sustainability into the future.

That is the essence of the social contract.

What Is the Social Contract?

You probably never thought that philosophy course would hold any value for your day-to-day work and life. And yet, we're about to discuss how Hobbes, Locke and Rousseau can actually help you make your organization socially responsible (in a meaningful way), financially viable over the long haul (not just this quarter), and assist in planning for long-term opportunities.

All organizations (or large social structures) have a contract with society, including for-profit, government, education, and non-profit organizations. This is an implicit, assumed contract that boils down to an agreement wherein, as long as the products and services your organization provides do not deliver some form of harm in or to society, you may continue doing business with little to no outside interference. Businesses operating according to new business realities[30] recognize (a) that this contract exists and (b) the necessity to align their organizational processes, products, outputs, and outcomes with the terms of this social contract. As Faith Popcorn stated, "doing good is no longer an option—it's a must."[31]

The concept of the "social contract" is based in-part on the argument that legitimate state authority is derived from the consent of the governed. In essence, we as individuals consent to give up some rights and let a larger social structure do its thing in return for obtaining benefits from that structure. This was originally conceived in governmental terms—we, the people, agree to give up some rights to let a governmental structure make decisions and maintain social order so long as the individuals reap the benefits of that larger social structure. Over time, this same concept has been applied to many other large social structures—big business, educational institutions and systems, and even entire professions such as medicine, education or law. We, the people, will allow you to do business, teach our children, protect our families, heal our loved ones, study your discipline, build your airplanes, build our roads and bridges—with very little interference from us—so long as we can reap the benefits of those structures.

But what happens when "we the people" are not reaping benefits? What happens when loved ones are increasingly being denied healthcare because of the "business" of healthcare? What happens when we put our family in a faulty car or airplane that leads to death or injury? What happens when faulty construction or maintenance (or *both*) on an interstate highway leads to a collapse that kills dozens? What happens when children go to school, but year-by-year still don't learn basic math and problem solving skills? What happens when a large-scale natural disaster hits but no government agency—local, state, national or otherwise—gets food, water and reliable shelter to those affected in a reasonable timeframe?

Contractual Obligations

A breach of a social contract is what happens. When the social contract is broken, society steps back in to stop a business or government entity (or any other type of organization) from doing its business in a detrimental way. According to both Locke's and Rousseau's interpretation, this contract is only legitimate so long as it serves the general interest.[32] When the general interest is no longer served, though, the contract gets renegotiated to change the terms and ensure the general interest is served. Renegotiation happens through regulation, legislation, and re-organization.

Speaking to an audience on "Cradle to Cradle Design" about environmental impact, William McDonough, award-winning architect and designer in sustainability, put it this way—"When our organizational plans and designs lead to polluted rivers and neuro-carbons that literally affect our children's brains, society says back to those organizations, 'Wait a minute—we never gave you the right to kill. We'll tell you at what rate you can dispense death.' Perhaps it's time for a new design."[33]

One of the clearest signs of a breach of social contract is regulation that inevitably flows from breakdowns. The nature of the social contract is that society allows an entity to do its business so long as it is not detrimental and society reaps benefits. In exchange for the benefits you deliver, society stays out of your business. When your business becomes detrimental, however, that breach of contract means society gets involved. Usually, the way it gets involved is through regulation—environmental standards and regulations, Sarbanes-Oxley, Federal Sentencing Guidelines, and No Child Left Behind, for example.

Frankel states, "Society's granting of power and privilege to the professions is premised on their willingness and ability to contribute to social well-being and to conduct their affairs in a manner consistent with broader social values."[34] Regulation is the most direct statement that the larger society has lost faith in a profession's ability to regulate itself. When regulation happens, it is often burdensome, as systems whose business is *not* your business get involved to tell you how to do things. There is no doubt it is onerous—and not a position either side of the equation prefers. Professionals don't want outside entities telling them how to do things, and society really doesn't want to have to take care of things that professionals should. Indeed, the maintenance of the social contract is a defining characteristic of what separates a profession (and, therefore, professionals) from just a bunch of people doing things.

The collapse of the financial and housing markets in 2008 and 2009 highlight society's dependence upon professionals to handle their business responsibly, and challenges how we currently credential and regulate professionals with the power to bring down entire industries and economies. In a comparative analysis of how the United States and Iceland both handled the failure of major banks, Smalera observes that "Iceland's 320,000 citizens will be paying for the hubris of a few hundred of their own, who dubbed themselves 'investment bankers'...and America's 300 million citizens will be paying for the hubris of a few thousand of their own, who dubbed themselves 'investment bankers.'"[35] When professionals fail on a large scale, it is translated into a failure of a given profession. In the past, this has led to significant changes not just in business regulations or legislation but has also impacted the curricula students go through at colleges and universities. Davis tracked the "ethics book" in higher education across several professions—business, law, medicine, and engineering—in responses to large, visible public failures of these professions that engendered distrust and tighter regulation of both practices and education of future professionals. Not only did businesses and firms have to change their practices, but higher education also had to modify their approaches to demonstrate that they can graduate students with the desired professional qualifications.[36] Increasingly, surveys of hiring professionals reflect that ethics are among the most highly valued characteristics of applicants.[37] Indeed, the breakdown of an entire profession reflects a systemic failure, with failure points located not just within the industry but within the education counterparts as well.

Thinking of social responsibility in social contract terms can be very powerful *and* empowering—societal impact is a contract with society your organization manages. Whether you currently manage it well or poorly, you *do* have this contract and you *are* managing it (even if you are managing by neglect). So this contract can be managed well or poorly. Just like a contractor you work with through your organization, if you fail to meet your contractual obligations, that contractor will call you on those agreements. And just like the contractors you currently work with, greater opportunities can come from strong partnerships. Ian Davis, Worldwide Managing Director of McKinsey & Company, states, "It can help to view the relationship between big business and society as an implicit social contract—Rousseau adapted to the corporate world, you might say. This contract has obligations, opportunities, and advantages for both sides."[38]

Society's Commitment to You: WIIFM (What's In It For Me)

By managing this social contract well, you will both avoid burdensome regulations and continue to be able to do your business as the professional with little to no outside interference. In addition, by managing this particular contract well, you will reap many benefits.

As Davis notes, there are opportunities and advantages to this contract, not just obligations. So let's look at what's in it for you. A notable trend across all the work on socially responsible organizations and ethics in organizations is the continued demonstration of benefits to the organization. This is in part why social responsibility isn't charity (just an outflow from your business), but an actual business strategy where outflow generates inflow.

What you and your organization get out of this contract (no contract is one-sided):

- A sustainable business model that will keep you in business over the long-term (not just the short-term) because society will continue to invest in the benefits you provide (either buying your products or voting to continue funding your efforts).[39]

- Generation of opportunities and competitive advantages over other companies (such as stabilized workforce regions).[40]

- Positive publicity and positive image that will attract business to you and/or increase public confidence and trust in your organization (rather than negative publicity that will drive business away or lead to widespread public dissatisfaction—think "the Tylenol effect" rather than "the Pinto effect").

- Higher rates of productivity and stronger job performance by your employees.[41]

- An ethical employee workforce—because organizations with a positive reputation for doing societal good and conducting themselves ethically attracts like-minded individuals who want to be a part of organizations that reflect their values.[42]

- Better selection and higher retention of talented, ethical employees (and therefore lower employee turnover) because organizations that demonstrate this sort of commitment also attract talent and enjoy high levels of employee loyalty.[43]

- Customer loyalty—Hatcher reports that "almost 100 percent of the population wants companies to focus on social responsibility more than profits and over 50 percent of the respondents said they form an impression of a company based on its social responsiveness, or lack thereof."[44]

As Grajew states it, this is "the advantage of doing the right things."[45] When you and your organization do the right things, you put the horse before the cart and get your organization moving in a strong direction. And people both inside and outside your organization want to be a part of your momentum—they like being a part of your organization, and they feel good about the work they are doing. These benefits are well-documented in much of the human resources literature.[46] Employees stay longer, are more productive, are more innovative, and express higher satisfaction with their jobs and companies.

This also gives your organization a long-term, strategic advantage. People will want to bring you their business or vote to allocate funds to your organization. As Oakley-Browne states, "If we add value to society in the long term, we will gain customer loyalty and stay in business for the long term."[47] Every company depends on people, and when people are treated well they respond positively. Grajew states, "It's an opportunity to have talents in your company, to have people engaged and committed, to have support from the community, support from consumers—in short, all the competitive advantages for a business."[48]

Your Deliverables: Measuring Societal Outcomes of Your Organization

As with any well-developed contract, it is critical to state just what the final deliverables will be, and to have clear indicators against which your organization can determine whether that contract has been fulfilled. In other words, it is critical to articulate the measurable outcomes that will result from your outputs, and then collect that data (get the facts).

Earlier, I defined social responsibility as *a way of gearing your organization towards delivering desirable societal outcomes in a manner recognizing that what you do, produce and deliver has an impact on society.* Social responsibility has so much more potential as a strategic course of action than as a marketing tagline. While the tagline feels nice right now, and makes for some great commercials and heart-warming reports, those don't lead to long-term viability and strategic opportunities that strengthen your organization's contract with society. For example, do you do business with global partners who treat their employees humanely, thus increasing self-sufficiency and decreasing poverty or discrimination? Or do your global partners have safe business practices and quality check standards (e.g., no lead paint on toys)? Does your school graduate students who recycle a lot but illegally download copyrighted music and photos?

The real value of a socially responsible organization comes from how social responsibility is defined in measurable (real) terms and integrated into strategic planning (for any type of organization). By identifying specific, desired societal outcomes for which your organization is responsible, you outline your contractual obligations with society. These are the ways in which your organization makes a difference in society—the ways in which stakeholders (not stockholders) are relying on you to reap the benefits of letting you do your business.

Dale Brethower states, "If you're not adding value to society, you're subtracting it."[49] Bottom line is that your organization impacts society—now it's time to plan for what you want that impact to be. Does what you do add up to the whole in a desirable way?

One aspect of social responsibility that has gained a lot of attention and support in recent decades is environmental impact and sustainability. That is certainly one of many socially-significant measures for which an organization can plan and get the facts, but there are others.

In his book *Mega Planning,* Kaufman outlines 13 measures of social responsibility that can be tracked over time. Those measures have been developed with organizations of varying size, including many names you would recognize, across different cultures and contexts. The result has been a culturally-independent definition of social responsibility that, when tested, has shown very high levels of statistical validity and reliability.[50] He has termed this collection of societally-referenced results an "Ideal Vision."

Kaufman's 13 measures are 13 outcomes—13 different types of socially responsible destinations that we design our organizations toward. We will cover those measures and Kaufman's model, and examine case studies around many of these measures across *all* types of organizations. We'll look at the levels of performance (Mega, Macro, and Micro—the three levels of planning and results based on Kaufman's Organizational Elements Model[51])—and how to draw alignment between the everyday actions and decisions of employees to the desired outcomes, especially socially significant outcomes, of your organization.

Your organization will not own all 13 of these socially-significant outcomes, but it does own a part of that pie. Your organization is a part of the whole. By identifying the ways your organization has an impact in the lives of individuals and society, and strategically planning toward the desired impact, you actually ensure your long-term viability. Your organization can become a part of the solution rather than a part of the problem—by design.

(And pssst...people like giving their money to, voting for, and working for organizations that are a part of the solution rather than a part of the problem.)

The Societal Value-Added Framework

A significant paradigm shift for organizational planning is the societal value-added frame of mind.[52] What this means is that you adopt a framework for your organization that recognizes how your organization is a subsystem within society, including your organization's impact on society, and says you want your organization to add value to society rather than detract from it, and you commit to plan towards that desired impact and get the facts on your progress. Rather than social good being a tangential, feel-good bonus that may or may not result, it is a recognition that everything you and your organization does, produces and delivers is aligned to achieve agreed-upon societal results. This is a shift from focusing on individual performance, or just the small circles inside your organization, to ensuring that you add value to external clients and society.

This does *not* mean you have to transform your organization into an engine for a social purpose. Indeed, the most influential of organizations today are not those with a social purpose, but with a financial purpose—big business. While delivering products, outputs, and services to markets that consumers want and demand, businesses (and "big business" collectively) are in a position to dramatically impact the shape of society and its future. According to Oded Grajew, a leading Brazillian toy manufacturer who created the Instituto ETHOS for socially responsible business in Brazil, the business sector is the most powerful sector in society. He states,

> "Of the hundred greatest economies in the world, 51 are businesses—the media, television, radio, newspapers in all the world are basically in the hands of the private sector... The private sector also has great political, electoral power. No one is unaware of the power of the private sector in elections. So, clearly, the situation we have today in the world, the situation of great disparity between rich and poor, of great environmental threat to the human species—clearly, those with so much power bear much responsibility for the world we have today."[53]

Your organization has a contract with society, and as part of that contract your agreement is to add value to society. So let's articulate that contract. In this chapter, we will begin with a general acknowledgment and articulation of the contract.

Use the following statement as the beginning part of your contract with society. This will help you focus your organization on truly socially responsible planning and set the framework for how you design towards desirable results—ethical results. This is where you start to define exemplary performance.

Your Organization's Social Contract

We commit to deliver organizational results that add value for all external clients and society. We recognize that our organization is part of the larger society, and therefore is an active partner in identifying and delivering desirable societal outcomes that result from our services and products. We are committed to getting the facts on the outcomes and tracking our success over time. We individually and collectively choose and commit to design our organization in a manner that clearly accomplishes desired outcomes for external clients and society, desired results for our organization, and desired performance within our organization. I commit, as an individual, to work individually and together to achieve this.

Signed by you, in representation of your organization

Articulating the Whole Contract

In this chapter, we covered a new way of thinking about social responsibility as not just a marketing campaign but an actual strategic plan. We highlighted the social contract that every business is already engaged in so you can manage this contract more effectively. In future chapters, we will fill in the details of that contract for different types of organization. By the end of this book, you should have a contract that:

(1) Acknowledges your organization's contract with society, (Chapter 1).

(2) Commits to add value to society, (Chapter 1).

(3) Identifies measurable societal outcomes that your organization contributes to (Chapter 2).

Endnotes

1. While this particular quote came from a 2007 news story on blow-outs of tires made by Hangzhou Zhongce Rubber, a Chinese manufacturer who sold the tires through Foreign Tire Sales (FTS) in New Jersey, the real commentary is how ubiquitous such a statement is across a number of news stories. Most would probably assume it comes from stories on the Firestone and Bridge-stone recall of 2000, when 6.5 million tires were recalled after 148 deaths and over 500 injuries were attributed to faulty tires (tread separation). http://www.consumeraffairs.com/news04/2007/06/china_tires03.html. The 2007 recall was issued on 450,000 of the Chinese-manufactured tires on the heels of at least two deaths and other injuries attributed to the tires. http://www.foreigntire. com/ documents/ Consumer%20release%20Final%20WORD.pdf. It turned out that the manufacturer decided to leave out gum strips that would have prevented the separation, contrary to their agreement with the auto dealer.

2. Valdes-Dapena, Peter. "Toyota: Saved $100 million dodging recall." CNN–Money. February 22, 2010.

3. Estes, 1996 and Lee, 2003, p. 73

4. Ibid

5. Bernárdez, 2005; Harrington, 1991; Kaufman, 1997, 2000; Kaufman, Oakley-Browne, Watkins, & Leigh, 2003; Pava, & Krausz, 1995

6. If you absolutely must insist that "conventional wisdom" is that the "business of business is business," then I would suggest you do yourself a favor and read Bernardez' article "Minding the business of business: tools and models to design and measure wealth creation" (2008). Bernardez does an excellent job explaining how "conventional planning" based solely on the single bottom line (profit) actually creates a cycle of boom and bust that makes it hard to distinguish quality organizational planning from good ideas and even scams. It may sound good to people who want to avoid accountability, but for real businesses that want to be viable, attention to two bottom lines is requisite. Businesses MUST be able to explain basic business concepts such as how they deliver continuing and measurable value to clients—other-wise, the lack of that clarity should be a red flag to investors and

consumers alike. Bernárdez has developed a "business case" model that incorporates both conventional and societal (Mega) criteria for both ethical and pragmatic planning and management in Bernárdez, M. (In Press). Sailing the Winds of "Creative Destruction:" Educational Technology during economic downturns. *Educational Technology.*

7.   Sarbanes-Oxley Act: http://frwebgate.access.gpo.gov/cgi-bin/ getdoc.cgi?dbname=107_cong_public_laws&docid=f:publ204.107 . Also Davis, 1999 and Hammond, 1992.

8.   Petrick & Scherer, 2003 and Sample, 2007

9.   Bernárdez, 2005

10. Drucker, 1984, 1989, 1995; see also Kaufman & Moore, in press, for details on how an ideal vision for society drives strategic planning.

11. Bernárdez, 2005—p.38

12. Kaufman, 2000, 2006

13. Davis, 2005

14. Brethower is also fond of saying, "In God we trust, all others must provide data."

15. The discussion here will use the three levels of results—Outcomes, Outputs, and products—suggested by Kaufman, 2006a, b in order to link and align three levels of planning and results. While these terms are not used universally, I suggest that they make a critical distinction that are important for Ethics by Design.

16. http://www.cbsnews.com/stories/2007/11/13/cbsnews_investigate s/main3496471.shtml, accessed December 18, 2007, "Suicide Epidemic Among Veterans" by Armen Keteyian, filed Nov. 13, 2007

17. 2007, http://www.va.gov/OCA/testimony/hvac/071212IK.asp

18. CBS News Transcript, Dec. 13, 2007—"Congress investigation suicide rates among veterans" from The Early Show on CBS, filed by Susan McGinnis.

19. Davis, 2005

20. Dobni, Ritchie & Zerbe, 2000; Kaufman, 1997, 2000, 2006; Verschoor, 1998.

21. Dobni, Ritchie & Zerbe, 2000; Kaufman, 1997, 2000, 2006; Verschoor, 1998.

22. http://www.msnbc.msn.com/id/21149977/—original documents and recall announcements were downloaded from Topps Meat website (www.toppsmeat.com) which has now become a generic website and no longer links to the recall documents.

23. National Education Association. "Code of Ethics of the Education Profession," 1975. Retrieved Oct. 24, 2008, http://www.nea.org/aboutnea/code.html

24. Drucker, 1984, 1989, 1995; Porter & Kramer, 2002. Also Kaufman 1972, Kaufman 2000, Kaufman, Oakley-Browne, Watkins & Leigh, 2003, Kaufman 2006.

25. von Bertalanffy, 1951, 1969

26. Rogers, 2003—Rogers is considered the father of diffusion of innovations theory. It should be noted that his theory is based on communications theory, not systems theory, which may explain the absence of system-level treatment in the model. However, since his work is very frequently cited and used for facilitating change, this lack of systemic treatment should be noted without detracting from the insights gained from the diffusion line of research.

27. Drucker, 1984, 1989, 1995; Bernardez, 2005; Kaufman, 1998, 2000

28. Drucker, 1989; Peters & Waterman, 1982; Prahalad & Hammond, 2002; see also "change creation" instead of "change management" as one of the new realities for business—Lick & Kaufman, 2000; Kaufman & Lick, 2000-2001.

29. 2000, 2006

30. See Bernardez, 2006; Kaufman, 2000, 2006; Kaufman & Guerra-Lopez, 2008; Kaufman in particular has collected a set of "new realities for planning" into a composite picture of what forward-thinking planning really means.

31. Popcorn, 1991

32. Lock, 1989; Rousseau, 1762; Hobbes, 1651

33. McDonough, 2006—in a podcast available from Stanford on iTunesU. For more, also see McDonough's book *Cradle to cradle: Rethinking the way we make things* (published in 2002 by North

Point Press in New York). McDonough explains how the current mindset for materials use and manufacturing is a linear model ending in waste. Recycling, while good in concept, is more like an accommodation to a broken system, and what's really necessary is a new paradigm for thinking in which "waste" is not part of the planned cycle. This underscores a predominant theme from much of the emerging literature around social responsibility: the outcomes must be planned for and designed towards rather than assumed.

34. Frankel, 1989, p. 110

35. Smalera, Paul. "Welcome to the United States of Iceland." March 11, 2010. CNN-Money. http://money.cnn.com/2010/03/10/news/international/Iceland_debt.fortune/. Accessed March 15, 2010.

36. Davis, M. 1999.

37. Procario-Foley, E. & D. Bean, 2002.

38. Davis, 2005

39. Drucker, 1985; Volcker, Norris & Bockelman, 2000

40. Porter & Kramer, 2006

41. Delaney & Sockell, 1991

42. Spector, 2006; Dobne, Ritchie, & Zerbe, 2000

43. HR Focus, 2006; Sample, 2007

44. Hatcher, 2002, p. 4

45. Grajew, 2007

46. Martinez, 1998; McNerney, 1996; Weiss, 1998

47. Oakley-Browne, 2007, p. 3—this comes from a personal communication in which Oakley-Browne shared a draft of a book—still in development.

48. Grajew, 2007—Stanford podcast

49. Brethower, 2006

50. Moore, 2005

51. Kaufman, 2000, 2006a, b

52. Kaufman & Guerra-Lopez, 2008

53. Grajew, 2007—Stanford podcast

Chapter 2
Socially Desirable Ends

"If you're not sure where you're going, you're liable to end up someplace else."

Robert Mager[1]

"If you can't define it, you can't improve it."

Ryan Watkins[2]

The Difference between Ends and Means

Confusing ends and means can be lethal. We can observe that in the area of social responsibility that has often lacked clear definition. Many fine organizations and institutions have headed down a path towards something, while not being quite sure what it is they're after. We care—we know we want to make a positive difference. We've just lacked clear definition. Many complex, vague concepts—like "diversity" and "caring" and "quality"—pervade mission statements and organizational goals or objectives that sound well-intentioned, but lack a clear destination. However, when we begin to think about social responsibility in terms of *consequences* (desirable or undesirable ends) and means for reaching those ends, we can actually clarify this seemingly-abstract topic.

So let's start by getting one thing clear—the difference between ends and means. This distinction makes a major difference when planning to deliver socially desirable outcomes by adding value to our shared society.

Ends are "results, achievements, consequences, payoffs, and/or impacts."[3] Ends are the consequences of actions and products. The output of your production line may be a tire which is delivered to market. The consequence (outcome) of that tire once it goes to market is safety, or, unhappily, possible lack thereof (i.e., injury, death, or property damage). If the product you deliver is sound, then the consequence is safety and long-wear. If the product you deliver is not high enough quality, the consequences are accidents that injure or kill customers (even non-customers on the road with your customers) and damage property.

Ends are defined in the form of objectives that are clear and measurable, so it is unmistakable when those objectives have been met. These clear, measurable, objectives address different levels across an organization, but regardless of the level, the objectives focus on clear results.[4]

Means are "processes, activities, resources, methods, or techniques used to deliver a result."[5] These are the strategies, solutions, actions, products, and processes we develop to reach a desired end. Your manufacturing line, for example, is a means for producing tires. Or your classroom is a means for producing future professionals and/or practitioners. However, means are very frequently mistaken for ends unto themselves. When this happens, an organization gets lost in doing things right instead of doing the right things. It can do a lot of things and still not be accomplishing desired results. The organization can even be doing a lot of things very well and win national honors or professional awards—and still not reach desired results.

This ability to distinguish ends from means, and then identify clear ends—a results orientation—distinguishes successful managers and leaders.[6] Oakley-Browne notes that studies which compare star performers in executive ranks to average ones find certain classic drive-for-results behaviors among the star performers, including the following:

- They set challenging, even audacious at times, objectives.

- They take the initiative and are self-directed towards their objectives.

- They identify personal and world (external) barriers to their objectives, and develop responses to overcome them.

- They seek feedback on progress towards their objectives.

- They are proactive, persistent and developed detailed action plans.

Strong leaders understand the value of objectives, and they set very clear objectives that focus on desired results. The value of objectives lies in how they are linked to consequences. Hugh Oakley-Browne explains that "Antecedents are like triggers or activators for performance."[7] Objectives are the ante-cedents to all the actions that take place in an organization—they trigger performance. Depending on how well-developed these objectives are, they can trigger poor performance or good performance. Thus, to accomplish desirable social results, you have to establish well-developed objectives.

The logic of a results focus is quite simple and sensible. First, you identify current results and then articulate the desired results. Then, you select the means for accomplishing those ends. No means are selected until the desired ends have been articulated first.

Let's practice separating ends from means so we can clearly separate results from the strategies that help us accom-plish results.

For each item listed, place a check mark in either the Ends column or the Means column, depending on whether it is pri-marily an end (result) or means (method or strategy).

Is this item an end, or is it a means for accomplishing something else? A good way of distinguishing is asking "so what" of everything you think is an end. So what if that hap-pens—does that lead to something? Are you doing that to accomplish something else? Are you just checking a task off your to-do list, or are you accomplishing something? (Answers are at the end of this chapter.)

Many of items in the activity are common statements in planning documents in organizations of all types, everywhere. However, just because they are common practice does not mean they are good practice. Some of these are even measur-able, but just being measurable doesn't make it a good objec-tive. In many of the instances above, the assumption is that doing those things will lead to something. Objectives clearly define that "something" these actions/solutions will lead to—the desired ends.

Item	Ends	Means
Train our staff on diversity		
Graduation		
Assessing needs		
Reorganization		
Policies on workplace diversity		
Positive credit rating		
Death/injury		
Increased communication between IT and other departments		
Reduce welfare funding		
Increased attention to student needs		
Benchmarking		
Increase prison funding		
Decrease class size		
Performance or merit-based pay increases		
Learning problem solving		

Once you can distinguish between ends and means, then you can begin to articulate current ends (where are you now) and desired ends (where you want to be). That discrepancy between current and desired ends, so valuable for defining and delivering desired and ethical results, is the basis for doing a useful needs assessment.

As Kaufman puts it, "calling something an 'end' doesn't make it one" (2000, p.43). Just because we are used to seeing these stated as "objectives" does not mean we should accept the poor practice. And the mere fact that something is measurable (e.g. decrease class size) does not mean it is an objective—decreasing class size is a means for accomplishing an end (it's usually assumed this will lead to increased student performance as measured by standardized tests). In many of these instances, the items sound good or make for great sound bites for politicians, but they may not actually accomplish the desired end. Pre-selecting means before you identify a clear, desired end usually leads to you doing things without accomplishing things (i.e., you may do things right but not be doing the right things).

Defining Desired Ends

We design solutions or plans that move us from a current end to a desired end. The presence or absence of clearly-stated desired ends in our designs makes a difference in whether we end up where we want to go or "someplace else."

Ends are the start points and end points in planning. Means are just that—our means for traversing the distance between a start point and an end point. We can only select *effective* means once we are clear on where we're headed.[8]

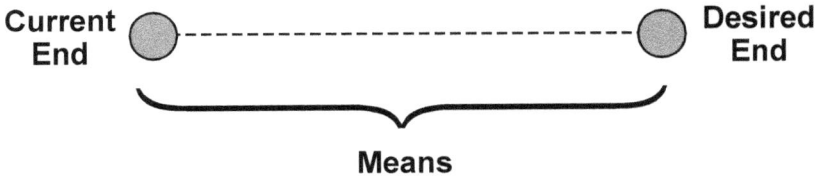

Current End ⚪--------------------------------⚪ **Desired End**

Means

In common practice, however, planning often winds up looking like this:

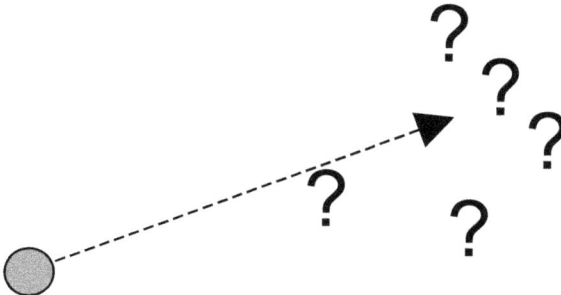

It's headed somewhere...it's just not clear where, and may not be clear until it's too late to get the ship turned around.

For example, a manager of training decides to implement an online training program that integrates blogs and wikis because he heard a lot of exciting presentations on it at the recent conference. Or, senior management decides "diversity" should be addressed in the organization, so they ask the training department to develop a series on diversity (never mind that "diversity" is often poorly defined itself).

This type of planning can be heard in decision statements made nearly every day in meeting rooms and offices around the country, from schools to businesses:

> "I've gotten several complaints on our services to students, so I'm going to get our staff some training on customer service."

> "My students didn't score so well on their last reading comprehension assessment, so I'm going to give them a few more books to read this week."

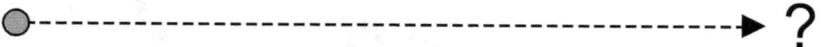

> "We don't seem to be getting as many sales as I thought we would, so let's do a marketing campaign."

⊙--------------------------------------➤ **?**

"I've gotten several complaints on our services to graduate students...   so I'm going to get our staff some training on customer service."

⊙--------------------------------------➤ **?**

"My students didn't score so well on their last reading comprehension assessment...   so I'm going to give them more books to read this week."

⊙--------------------------------------➤ **?**

"We don't seem to be getting as many sales as I thought we would,   so let's do a marketing campaign."

While these all start with a current end state, none of them include a desired end state. So it's not clear where any of these are headed, only what they're doing. Without that defined end, it's not clear if these means will get folks where they want to go. Effective planning looks more like the following.

Current End   **Desired End**

About half of my students read   I want all my students to score at
at about 80% accuracy on their   least 90% accuracy on the next
last reading comprehension   reading assessment within one
assessment.   month.

---►

Means

Based on their error patterns, I can tell most of them had problems with sight words (*needs analysis*). I will do more sight word practice in class, and provide them with opportunities for practice (*tactic*).

Current End   **Desired End**

Our security department has   Our security department will
received 15 complaints about   have a record of no discrimina-
racial profiling in the last 3   tion against any group of society
months.   based on age, gender, race, or
                                           other irrelevant factors as indi-
                                           cated by the number of substan-
                                           tiated and upheld complaints be-
                                           ing zero by this time next year.

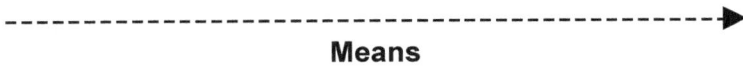

---►

Means

If the problem appears to be a particular individual (*needs analysis*), we will put that individual in a different position or replace the individual. If the problem appears to be pervasive, we will revise procedures, present this data to the staff, and track incidents over time publicly, review poorly-handled incidents, and provide training on proper procedures, incorporate effective procedures into employee evaluations, and remove individuals as a last resort, if necessary.

These are pretty complex examples, but so are the realities of organizations. So trying to over-simplify effective planning has led to poorly defined objectives and poor results and consequences. The work comes on the front-end in these examples, rather than continually having to re-do poorly planned activities.

Note in particular what the clearly-defined desired ends entail. These are measurable—you will know whether the end has been achieved. They are very clear on who will achieve the objective, to what degree (criterion), by when, and as measured by what. In the next chapter, we'll go into great detail on articulating effective objectives with examples of objectives for socially desirable ends for all types of organizations.

Values Statements vs. Value Added: Key to Ethics by Design

For a long time, we have not included *socially desirable ends* in our plans. McDonough explains, " ...it's no longer acceptable for us to say this isn't part of our plan...because it's part of our *de facto* plan. It's the thing that's happening because we have no other plan. Then we realize as a culture that we have become strategically tragic."[9] By not defining these ends, we deliver a future and a world to our children that are unintentionally tragic, and potentially irreversible.

Thus, it is crucial to articulate clear ends so we can plan and design towards these desirable ends. And those ends must be both useful and ethical.

Ethics are often addressed (if addressed at all) in organizations through statements—such as values statements or codes of ethics. However, the results of these exercises often reflect the core beliefs and values of the individuals at an organization. Part of the problem with using core beliefs and values of individuals is addressed later in this chapter. The real drawback to addressing ethics only through values statements or codes of ethics is that they are often just window dressing—something someone may point to as evidence of ethics in an organization, when really they're just evidence that something got written down. Often, core beliefs and values are statements of means and intentions and don't provide useful ends. Values statements and codes of ethics by and large do not influence performance—of the organization or of employees within the organization.[10]

When ethics are defined as performance—or results—not just philosophies or values, a whole new approach to ethics opens up. Research on leadership and organizational performance repeatedly demonstrates that clearly defining performance expectations is key to exemplary performance (any sort). Ethics are actually a way of defining exemplary performance. And when viewed as a form of performance, we then see how we can develop clear performance expectations around ethics, just as we define clear performance expectations around other types of performance.

Thus, there is a difference between simply stating what you value versus stating what value your organization adds and how your employees contribute to adding that value. If you really desire ethical performance within and from your organization, you have to define ethics in performance terms. By making the shift from values statements to a value-added framework, you shift the focus from vague statements to clearly defined ends. The value-added framework is all about defining precisely what value your organization adds and, thus, is about defining clear performance expectations by articulating the desired outcomes of your organization. This is how you translate ethics from stating ethics to *doing* ethics.

Let's take a look now at a model of socially desirable ends. These socially desirable ends are a part of the implicit social contract you manage—they are the value you add or subtract from society.

Socially Desirable Ends

As addressed in detail in the first chapter, your organization has an impact on external clients and society. Whether you acknowledge this impact or not is irrelevant to the fact of it. However, when you acknowledge this impact, you can begin to plan for desired impact—this planning is how you manage the social contract your organization has with society. These societal ends are the deliverables of your contract with society.

Socially responsible planning comes down to defining and designing the ideal world. Recall the section on system thinking in Chapter 1—what do we want the whole to look like? Based on that, you determine how your organization contributes to those ideal results. (Keep in mind, you already contribute or detract from those results—we're just planning *intended* results.) This act of defining and designing the ideal world is precisely how you accomplish ethics *by design*. A design is an expression of intention towards a desired end. When socially desirable results become a part of that defined, desired end, then our resulting designs are the means by which we accomplish those ends.

Do we want a safer world where you would put your own family in the car you manufacture, and therefore want every other parent to feel safe putting their children in the car you build? Do we want a world of equal opportunities where any person can become self-sufficient, regardless of social status, race, gender, phase of life, sexual preference, or other surface-level (irrelevant) characteristics? Do you want your children to live in a society free of war, terrorism, and riot and not be subjugated to poverty and slave-like conditions, and therefore ensure that the way you conduct business or your business partners don't subject other families or children to that sort of life and conditions?

Just what is the world we want our children to inherit? Every activity and product of every organization is an act of creating that future—for better or for worse. Do we leave a debt to our children and grandchildren, or do we leave them an investment? Thomas Jefferson provided sage advice when he argued that the debts of a generation should never be passed down to the next generation. He stated,

> *"...the earth belongs in usufruct to the living*: that the dead have neither powers nor rights over it...no man can, by *natural right*, oblige the lands he occupied, or the persons who succeed him in that occupation, to the payment of debts contracted by him. For if he could, he

might during his own life, eat up the usufruct of the lands for several generations to come; and then the lands would belong to the dead, and not to the living"[11]

By beginning with socially desirable ends, we plan our organizations in such a manner that we do not pass social debts along to future generations.

Kaufman and colleagues have worked with organizations of all types around nearly the entire world—from Singapore to India to Australia to the United States of America to Mexico, and many others in between—and with different types of organizations including large corporations, federal and state government entities, educational institutions and national militaries.[12] Over time, Kaufman developed the Basic Ideal Vision—a measurable definition of what people all around the world, regardless of religion or culture or background, want to create as the world tomorrow's child will inherit.

To derive these societal ends, Kaufman asked people "What kind of world, in measurable terms, do you want to help create for tomorrow's child?" Kaufman notes, "It is fascinating, and satisfying, to notice how much agreement there is, even across diverse cultures, about the ideal world and Ideal Vision for all organizations and individuals to move toward. By asking people about their children and grandchildren, and not about themselves, there is a willingness to be idealistic as well as realistic."[13]

The result over the years is the following Basic Ideal Vision, stated in measurable terms.

Basic Ideal Vision: The world we want to help create for tomorrow's child.

There will be no losses of life nor elimination or reduction of levels of well-being, survival, self-sufficiency, and quality of life from any source, including (but not limited to):

- War and/or riot and/or terrorism
- Unintended human-caused changes to the environment including permanent destruction of the environment and/or rendering it nonrenewable
- Murder, rape, or crimes of violence, robbery, or destruction to property
- Substance abuse
- Disease
- Pollution
- Starvation and/or malnutrition
- Destructive behavior, including child, partner, spouse, self, elder, and others
- Discrimination based on irrelevant variable including color, race, age, creed, gender, religion, wealth, national origin, or location

Poverty will not exist, and every woman and man will earn at least as much as it costs them to live unless they are progressing toward being self-sufficient and self-reliant. No adult will be under the care, custody, or control of another person, agency, or substance. All adult citizens will be self-sufficient and self-reliant as minimally indicated by their consumption being equal to or less than their production.

(Taken from Kaufman, 2000, p. 95, 2006)

This model has been tested and has demonstrated a strong internal structure as well as a high reliability.[14]

Overcoming resistance. Some common early arguments or resistance to this Basic Ideal Vision included concerns that it disregards culture, doesn't ask people about their core values or beliefs, or that it assumes these are the same for everyone. Let's deal briefly with each of these, assuming you may be wondering the same thing. Then we'll get into how these are measurable, what part of the whole your organization impacts, and some case studies.

First, these ends or consequences are culturally independent—in other words, they don't change across cultures. Environmental damage is environmental damage, whether it's happening in the US, China, Malaysia, Iceland or anywhere else. The question of whether it is valued is irrelevant to the very real consequences. Much the same with the other measures—war is war regardless of what culture you are in. Death is death; injury is injury; illness is illness.

These are universally-relevant outcomes for any culture, and this helps highlight the difference between "ethics" that focus on what you value (or what our organization or community values) and ethics that focus on what value you add. As we come to understand what it truly means to be in a global society, with a systemic understanding of interrelated results where one action here produces an outcome there, it becomes far more critical to focus on what we have in common.

Where culture comes in—and is *highly* relevant and critical—is *how* these ends or consequences are accomplished. A company in the United States can commit to decrease damage to the environment, and a company in India can make the same commitment. How they both get there, though, can vary when they take culture and contextual considerations into account. The end result is still increased or decreased damage to the environment—their means for doing so, though, are what's different. Thus, as Kaufman explains, culture is about means, not ends.

The same holds true when asking people about their core values or beliefs. Beliefs and values are even more individualized than culture, and thus vary (of course) from person to person. Many strategic planning frameworks suggest starting with partners' core values and beliefs as a starting point. However, beliefs and values tend to be more about means and resources and can be unexamined and strongly held even in the face of contrary evidence.[15] For example, a group of individuals that starts with the strongly-held belief that technology is beneficial will go straight to technological solutions (means) before identifying what ends they're trying to accomplish. It is also possible, and likely, to have involved individuals whose core values or beliefs are actually contrary to future societal good. Even in the United States, it is possible to have individuals involved who do not value diversity—and yet to build those core values into a strategic plan would actually lead to increased discrimination both inside and outside the organization. These are not desired results, even if they are aligned with core values.

The argument that these cannot be assumed for everybody hinges primarily on the two concerns already addressed. Such a stance tends to focus on culture or differences in values, beliefs, or definitions of "truth" and "reality." While these differences are very real, again, these differences are about means. In reality, we have a shared, systemically interrelated, global society in which actions here lead to results there. Discarding old, unwanted computers from the United States into third-world countries leads to illness as people are exposed to toxic chemicals. The interrelated nature of the world actually calls upon us to start *first* with our similarities—what we share in common. And what we do share in common, based on the work of Kaufman and colleagues, is a desire to create an ideal (as well as practical and ethical) world for our children and grandchildren. Regardless of culture or religion or values, nearly all of us want our children to grow up in a world where there is no war or riot, death, injury, illness, discrimination, abuse, pollution, environmental damage, or substance abuse, and in which every person on the planet can be self-sufficient. *How* we get to this ideal world will vary across cultures and continents—but the definition of that ideal world appears stable as a thread that unites humanity.

Society, when grappling with the very real consequences of an organization's failures, is not concerned at all with the values and beliefs of that organization but instead questions what value that organization adds to or subtracts from society. Thus, this model shifts the focus from those inside the organization to the impact of the organization on those outside of it.

The elements of the Basic Ideal Vision are the uniting threads, or variables—they are the things we all *as humans* care about regardless of culture, religion, or what type of organization we are working in. These elements are literally the ties that bind—that bind what your organization does, produces and delivers to society. It is only by addressing these that we build the shared world we desire. And these can only be addressed collectively by each diverse type of organization—business, government, education, military, etc.—taking on its slice of the whole.

The societal-level result—or end—of your organization's contributions or activities is one or more of the following 13 measures:[16]

1. War and/or riot and/or terrorism

2. Shelter

3. Unintended human-caused changes to the environment including permanent destruction of the environment and/or rendering it nonrenewable

4. Murder, rape, or crimes of violence, robbery, or destruction to property

5. Substance abuse

6. Disease

7. Pollution

8. Starvation and/or malnutrition

9. Child abuse

10. Partner/spouse/elder abuse

11. Accidents, including transportation, home, and business/workplace

12. Discrimination based on irrelevant variables including color, race, age, creed, gender, religion, wealth, national origin, disability, or location

13. Self-sufficiency:

  a) Poverty will not exist, and every woman and man will
     earn at least as much as it costs them to live unless
     they are progressing toward being self-sufficient and
     self-reliant.

  b) No adult will be under the care, custody or control of
     another person, agency, or substance. All adult citi-
     zens will be self-sufficient and self-reliant as mini-
     mally indicated by their consumption being equal to
     or less than their production.

Every one of these is a measurable result of one organization or another. Stated differently, your organization delivers
one or more of these results to society based on what you do,
produce and deliver.

This list tends to appear daunting to many folks at first.
However, the argument here isn't that your organization is
responsible or somehow affects all of these. Think of these
measures as the total composite of wellness/health of a global
society. Your organization impacts a part of that overall picture.
So while there may appear to be no real link between your
organization and spousal abuse, there may very well be a link
between health outcomes and the products you deliver, or your
stated organizational objectives and individuals' self-sufficiency.

Porter and Kramer[17] articulate a practical approach: identify
the points of intersection between your organization and society, and then select social issues that you should address that
rest at that point of intersection. There is a reciprocal relationship between the societal impact your organization has, and
the impact that improved social conditions have on your
organization. Porter and Kramer provide an example:

> "By addressing the AIDS pandemic in Africa, a mining
> company such as Anglo American would not only
> improve the standard of living on that continent; it
> would also improve the productivity of the African labor
> force on which its success depends"[18]

This is why true social responsibility is strategic planning, not philanthropy or a marketing tag line: there is a clear relationship between societal outcomes and your organizational results.

Socially Desirable Ends as a Definition of Accountability

In case the link to accountability isn't already clear, let's detail just how these define a framework for accountability as well as performance standards. Performance standards tend to be something an organization articulates for itself—whereas accountability tends to be standards that are externally defined by some entity, that a given profession or set of organizations are then held to and measured against.

Socially desirable ends are the ethical bases for accountability of social responsibility. The measures presented here are outcomes every organization delivers, and based on how your organization impacts these measures (do you increase or decrease deaths, or do you increase or decrease self-sufficiency?), society determines the relative value you are adding to their lives. By using these measures as an explicit framework, accountability for societal impact can cease being the squishy concept it usually is and become a clearly-defined framework. The benefit of working with a clearly-defined framework is that we are then able to develop a common language for discussing social responsibility and detailing how a given organization is adding or subtracting value from society.

For example, when homeowners are sent into foreclosure as a result of shady lending practices, ignorant buying decisions, and onerous terms for loans, this directly impacts self-sufficiency. When highway maintenance or assessment teams fail to address a deteriorating bridge structure, this directly impacts injuries, deaths, and accidents. When an industry continues to purchase goods (be it oil or coffee beans or raw materials) from a region where workers are subjected to unhealthy, polluting, abusive work situations, that industry (or individual companies) impact abuse, injury, self-sufficiency, and in some cases even war or riot.

When we get clear about those societal-level impacts, we also get clear about what we are going to hold each organization accountable for. It then becomes more straight-forward, as examples, for:

1. a consumer to identify which organizations they want to support with their purchasing power (dollars);

2. society or a regulatory body to determine what the desired impacts should be, and whether an industry is adding such desired value;

3. an organization to identify the specific ways in which their industry or individual organization impacts society, and therefore plan for the desired impact;

4. training grounds for professionals (trade schools, higher education, etc.) to integrate clearly defined social responsibility standards into their curricula;

5. offices or bodies of assessment to detail the societal-level impact of a given industry, organization, or decision.

Rather than defining accountability in process terms (e.g. banks are making loans available to millions of new homeowners they never would have before), we can now define accountability in impact terms (e.g. banks are making it possible for more families to purchase and keep their homes to establish a sound quality of life, wherein they can be self-sufficient).

Accountability is about more than just being a good steward or good corporate citizen. It actually is a distinguishing characteristic between quality organizational planning and organizations that either are poorly shaped or simply are scams to begin with. In dissecting the "conventional wisdom" of the single-bottom-line approach, Bernardez provides an excellent critique of precisely why a profit-only approach to planning is a recipe for on-going, drastic, systemic failures.

"The problem with (the single-bottom-line) approach—exemplified by the recurrence of Enrons, subprime mortgages and other scams window-dressed by these business cases' deceiving financial calculations—is that financial figures fail to explain *the business* in the "business case": how we create and deliver measurable and continuing value to the client, how much and how well our clients and their clients will do with our products and services. If a business case cannot explain convincingly these basic business concepts, a "*caveat emptor*" sign should "flag" investors about the risks they are assuming.

A more contemporary and accurate approach to define a business proposition comes from factoring, analyzing and monetizing research-based data about how products and services actually increase clients, clients' clients and market's revenues, resources and wealth, by adding a second "top line" that reflects clients and community revenue to the conventional income statement in order to determine where the money comes from and what kind of tangible benefits a client actually gets in exchange for what he/she paid.

This second top line measures not just profit extraction but value creation and renovation because it shows *how the company's products and services actually add value to clients, replace the natural resources utilized and strengthen the markets and communities that consume them*—something that would have set off the alarms at Enron when the company traders started to shut down Californian power utilities to gouge prices and sustain unrealistic return goals based on a purely financial business case made to gamble the stock market."

As Bernardez explains, by using conventional wisdom companies can make themselves look good on paper. If we follow just the profit trail, we will find ourselves sorely misled into even more Enrons and banking industry fallouts. By tracking performance on the second bottom line (which organizations are impacting whether they gather the data or not), investors and consumers alike are better able to separate the wheat from the chaff—to distinguish the organizations that are truly engaging in responsible business planning and those that are just trying to turn a quick profit at any expense. This, then, begins to provide a framework for accountability, leading to more informed decisions on which companies to invest in or divest from.

Let's study some cases to clarify that these socially desirable ends are real, measurable, and how they apply across a variety of organizations and industries.

Real-World Examples

Stolen iPods: Bad People or Bad Systems?[19]

110 million devices around the world (and counting), and one white-hot black market springing up behind it. iPod thefts are on the rise—around the country and the world. People have been injured and, in one case, killed—solely for an iPod.

In summer 2007, Dateline NBC decided to take on the burgeoning iPod theft rates and see just how easy it was to track a stolen iPod—and just what Apple could do and is or is not doing about it.

What they found was how quickly and easily iPods get stolen (not surprisingly), how people (at least in American culture) justify clearly unethical—and illegal—behavior, and how easy it is to track a stolen iPod. They also unveiled a public discussion on responsibility—who's responsible for your stolen iPod? Where does individual responsibility end and corporate responsibility begin?

All iPods are registered upon initial use and can, thus, be tracked back to individuals using personal information. In their

(continued)

Real-World Examples (continued)

investigation, Dateline NBC placed 20 iPods in different situations in public to see if they could track a stolen iPod. Dateline
managed to track down 12 of the 20 stolen iPods (a 60% recovery rate) using the same sort of information Apple collects when
devices are plugged into a computer and registered.

At first blush, this looks like a clear case of individual choices
over which no business has any control. How could a business
possibly be held responsible for individual thefts of devices?
Even the people who stole the devices appeared to reinforce
that the buck stops with them. One person caught by Dateline
admitted that he simply had bad judgment at that time.

However, the scope of the problem, increasing crime rates
surrounding the particular device, and the black market popping
up around it all point to a problem larger than bad individual
judgment.

John Reid, then a top government law enforcement official
from England, stated, "If I had one piece of advice, it actually
wouldn't be to young people, it would be to the manufacturers.
And that is: help us to design in features which reduce crime."

NYPD detective Richard Kenney echoed the role the company plays in reducing crime. When asked if the public knew
there was a way to track iPods, what would the impact be on
iPod theft, Kenney responded: "The people actually committing
the crimes and stealing them would stop doing that because
they won't have anyone to sell them to."

iPod theft has become a serious enough problem, even
according to Apple, that both consumers and law enforcement
are urging action on the part of Apple, and Apple has filed for a
patent related to security that would decrease crime rates.[20]
Apple is not legally responsible for the theft. However, they are
socially responsible for their portion of the system that contributes to the problem. And upon close examination, it becomes
evident that out of all the entities involved (business, law
enforcement, etc.), Apple is the key party that can best influence
the most significant portion of the social problem—consequences. They are clear about the measurable impact in their
patent filing: "This should result in a significant reduction of
crime against the lawful owner of such devices."

Recall the imagery in the beginning of the book—of marbles in a bowl, and when one marble shifts, the other marbles shift with it.[21] When a company introduces a new innovation (products, processes, or ideas) into society—which is the main reason most companies are in business—they shift the marbles in the bowl. That is the nature of change. That shift has to be assumed—that a shift will take place is a fact. However, most planning stops at the point of the creation of that new marble (or new innovation) added to the bowl. Truly strategic planning, though, accounts for the fact that a shift will take place in the bowl, and plans for a desirable outcome from that shift upon the other marbles and the bowl as a whole. As one engineer put it, engineers can't just sit in their offices and create something then lob it over the fence at society. If it has a negative impact, society will toss it back over and say, "No, Mr. Engineer. Try again."[22] Designs, including technological designs and innovation, have to take societal impact into consideration.

Let's examine the Apple iPod case to see just what that means. When Apple created the iPod and then delivered it to the market, at a very base level they made a lot of profit on a device that became an instant hit. The device had an obvious impact on the music industry (one subsystem of society) in terms of how music is packaged and delivered to listeners. However, it also impacted other parts of society (or other marbles in the bowl) like law enforcement (another subsystem of society). With the advent of the iPod came the advent of a black market for the device—creating an additional burden for law enforcement officials. iPods are hot and desirable. They are also very easy to steal and keep—made all the easier by a feature that's actually *missing*.

For all the many great features in iPods and the Apple system, they presently lack a key systemic design feature that drives behavior. System features could actually be the strongest deterrents to crime, reducing the crime rates and the likelihood that an individual is harmed or murdered over a device. A single system feature that deters crime could actually bring the black market for the devices to a halt, while also reducing the load on an already over-burdened law enforcement system *and* increase the perceived value of investing in a product that's well-protected by the company. That systemic feature is consequences.[23] A lack of consequences (good or bad) can significantly alter what individuals choose or do in a variety of situations, including their choices within an organization or in society at large. We'll look at systemic barriers such as consequences in more detail in Chapter 4 and relate those to ethics as a form of performance design.

For many centuries, ethics have focused on the individual—what choice does an individual make, what is the moral development of individuals (e.g. Kohlberg), what are different frameworks a person may use to work through their ethical reasoning (e.g. duty, virtue, utilitarianism, etc.). However, looked at from a performance perspective, research indicates that the vast majority of breakdowns in performance are not individual breakdowns but are system breakdowns. Only 10-20% of performance failures are individual problems. So 80-90% of breakdowns are due to system features; those features promote either poor (or undesirable) performance or promote exemplary performance.[24] With the systemic paradigm comes a new lens for viewing ethics—systemic ethics and systemic solutions or design features that drive ethics (one way or another).

Let's look at an education example.

Example: Educational Institution

"The simple truth is that what the schools do and what the schools accomplish is of concern to those who depend upon the schools, those who pay the bills and those who pass the legislation. We are not in a vacuum, and our results are seen and judged by those outside of the schools—those who are external to it....This external referent should be the starting place for functional and useful educational planning, design, implementation, and evaluations—if education does not allow learners to live better and contribute better, it probably is not worth doing, and will probably ending up being attacked and decimated by taxpayers and legislators."[25]

   While educational institutions often assume they are delivering a societal good, this is an assumption that really has to be
tested and backed by data. Again, if you care, get the facts.
Education administrators and professionals are under increasing pressure to make decisions based on data—from data-
based practices in classrooms to data-driven results and consequences.[26] We see the evidence in No Child Left Behind legislation, and in the way grant funding for schools and universities are evolving to an increased focus on hard-performance
data. Indeed, regulation of education is increasing—in the face
of vocal disappointment with what the education system has
delivered. *A Nation at Risk* continues to haunt our educational
institutions, questioning just what value the current design of
the school system adds to society.
   This is presently a heated contentious discussion across
educational organizations, in large part because it has been
(mis)translated into heavy-handed accountability that often
does not measure what really matters. The primary course for
educational organizations, and really for any organization, is to
reclaim accountability as something that aids these institutions
in gathering meaningful data, to include positive societal impact
data (rather than accountability becoming yet another process
to be "done right" that overburdens an educational system).
State and federal departments of education play a significant
part in this type of performance, as the way they implement
"accountability" to measure and oversee school/district performance focuses almost entirely on process-oriented compliance checklists rather than meaningful evaluation of progress
towards desirable end results. The true end clients—students,
and their future in society—often get lost amidst the checklists
that make sure pieces of papers or reports are getting turned
in, or standardized assessments are conducted, or plain poli-
tics. Philosophical debates on literacy approaches, or math
education, or second-language learners bog down an office or
department or school while the children still go to school every
day. They move and grow up even if the whole or parts of the
education system don't.

One example of an educational institution that got their boat turned towards impact on external clients (i.e., students) and society is the Instituto Tecnológico de Sonora (ITSON) in Sonora, Mexico. This example comes courtesy of Guerra & Rodriguez.[27] Like many public education institutions, ITSON has a mission that is focused on a commitment to society and public service. This is no different from the purpose of public education—K-12 and higher education—in the United States. These are public institutions, publicly funded, intended to serve the public at large and be a positive contributing factor to the local and national community.

Not Just Service Learning but Social Impact

In 1993, ITSON decided it wanted to add measurable value to its students, the academic community, and society and has been applying Kaufman's Mega Planning model to their institution for fourteen years and counting. And this is not just at an undergraduate or certification level—the model has been implemented all the way from a certification program to an undergraduate degree, to a Master's degree and a Doctorate degree. "The main driver of ITSON's planning model is the alignment of university deliverables to societal needs, as well as the international accreditation of the programs it offers" (p. 58). To accomplish this, ITSON mapped out a five phase, long-term process; the phases are as follows, including the timeframes for each phase:

1. **Planning:** reflection, raising awareness, education, redimensioning, structuring, evaluation, and negotiation (1991-1995)

2. **Implementation:** evaluation of milestones and en-route results, formative evaluation, improvement recommendations, and adjustments (1995-2001)

3. **Evaluation of Curricular Results:** selection of areas to promote towards levels of excellence in terms of social impact; redesign (2002-2008)

(continued)

Not Just Service Learning but Social Impact (continued)

---

4. **Evaluation of Social Impact:** globalization of educational programs, consolidation of institutional alignment, continuous improvement (2009-2015)

5. **Evaluation:** innovation, leadership through the integration and articulation of educational programs with economic and social organizations that support the sustainable development of the region (2015 forward)

Indeed, this reflects a true and deep commitment on the part of the institution towards adding measurable value to society, as well as a recognition that such a major change within the institution will take time to manage. Furthermore, once implemented, as with any good planning there is on-going attention to maintenance of what works and improvement or growth into additional areas.

ITSON's story does not stop at just a set of phases, though. By now they are well into the third phase and on the cusp of fourth-phase activities. Let's look at what ITSON did specifically at the curricular level, how that translates into alignment towards societal impact, and what their current data reflects in terms of impact.

Curricular design and alignment: ITSON evaluated the curricular model and in 2002 aligned the model with professional competencies expected of graduates. As a result, ITSON developed various Mega-oriented programs:

- **Integrated Community Development Program**

  As part of this program, professors and students from a range of academic departments work with local, rural communities around the state of Sonora to build various types of organizations that support the community and directly target a form of communal improvement in that area. Guerra and Rodriguez describe the state of Sonora as highly agricultural, whose major economies are cattle ranching, fishing, and mining. The region faces serious challenges such as unemployment, vandalism, disorganization, drug addiction, emigration, and lack of food supply, medical care, public safety, and technology. The

---

(continued)

Not Just Service Learning but Social Impact (continued)

area also has a significantly high dropout rate (p. 59). As a result of ITSON's efforts, Guerra and Rodriguez report that, in the course of a single year, 140 students from 14 different undergraduate programs, and 30 professors from 10 academic areas, together developed a total of 48 community projects. These projects span a host of disciplines. The actual breakdown of the projects reflects such a diverse approach:

- 14 in Educational Support
- 12 in Health
- 8 in Arts, Culture, and Sports
- 6 in Economic Development
- 4 in Infrastructure Assessment and Maintenance
- 4 in Technology Use

It should be noted that this is different from "service learning," a model of education gaining popularity in which students get involved in community projects to apply their university learning. While service learning *could* be directed at positive societal impact, the difference lies in whether the approach is targeted at a specific societal need and actually measures the impact of the student projects on the community. Without a data-based reason for the project and a data-driven approach to desired consequences, service learning is not a form of societal impact in higher education.

- **ITSON-Consulting**

  The goal of ITSON-Consulting is to provide advice to small and medium businesses in the state of Sonora that strengthens these businesses. As of the 2005 report, 103 companies had been assisted and 173 consultants trained, with 80 achieving certification. The areas of application included Market Research, Production, Administration, Human Resources, Finance, Quality and Ethics, and Culture.

- **Masters in Agribusiness**

  The primary goal of this program was to develop experts in agribusiness who could have a positive impact on the growth

(continued)

Not Just Service Learning but Social Impact (continued)

and development of agriculture and cattle in the area. The research plan for the program is based on specific problems in the region and identifies specific needs that form student projects and research. The Masters program began in 2003 with 13 projects, 20 students, and 8 faculty. There are four key concepts underlying the design of this program:

- *Learn by doing:* Students and faculty work with real clients looking to develop a business plan, allowing them to apply theory to practice and face real deadlines and expectations.

- *Funding center:* Clients actually fund the projects by providing materials and equipment.

- *Academic responsibility:* Each project has two deliverables—a case study that can be shared inside and outside the university, and a business plan with appropriate objectives and detail.

- *New academic paradigm:* Students and faculty share the learning experience—research is conducted cooperatively.

To date, the new learning paradigm has been adopted, and the community is benefitting financially from these efforts. The university has become a key contributor to development in the agricultural sector and also started to receive international recognition for their work and results.

- **Software Factory**

    ITSON also set out to develop the intellectual capital in the region, so in 2004 they launched the Software Factory. The goal of the Software Factory is to generate economic transformation in Sonora by essentially serving as an incubator for technology-based businesses. Projects started under the Software Factory include: Internet support system for education in the region; knowledge management; Centers for Strategic, Tactical, and Operational Information; support in the accreditation of educational programs; management of student tutoring; alumni tracking; virtual window for student, faculty, and staff services; library system.

(continued)

Not Just Service Learning but Social Impact (concluded)

- **Performance Improvement Institute**

    The Performance Improvement Institute currently has 20 independent sponsors all committing to maintain a Mega-focus. These sponsors are from the public as well as private sectors.

- **Ph.D. and MBA Programs**

    These programs are centered on Mega thinking and planning.

The following chart summarizes just how ITSON measured the value added at different planning levels, including societal impact (Mega). We will examine these three levels of planning in detail in Chapter 3.

Planning Level	Result	Some Indicators

Mega	Self-sufficiency/
	• self-reliance
	• quality of life (QOL)
	• Continued employment at C < P level
		• Optimal Employment (i.e., graduate working in the field for which he/she studied)—within 6 months of graduation
		
		• Earned Income trend over a seven-year period
		
		• Employer Satisfaction Index
		
		• Continued employment
		  – Local
		  – Out of town
		  – Income trend (slope)
		
		• Sub-employment

(continued)

		All further analyzed according to: – Gender – Age – Social/economic class – Father's occupation – Parent's education – Marital status – Single parent – Divorced – Disease, health
Macro	Graduation	• Graduation rates • Number of drop-outs (first year deserters) – Number of drop-outs who are making same or more than when they started • Number of non-completers (complete first two years) – Number of non-completers who are making same or more than when they started
Micro	Program Completion Course Completion	• Number of years for completion • Completion rate per program • Drop-out rate per program • Completion rate per course • Drop-out rate per course

(Taken from Guerra & Rodriguez, 2005)

While this is a higher education example, by no means should that be taken to imply that this cannot be applied in K-12 education. What this does imply for K-12 education is that we have to consider long-term impact data for schools and districts, as well as begin building long-term views into planning and funding (especially large federal funds and grants) to articulate precisely what the societal-level impact of educational initiatives should be. When schools perform well, the local communities perform well. Areas are seen as desirable for businesses, families want to move there, and the general health of the population is improved when school performance is high. These desired outcomes can be defined at the national, state, and local levels as part of a critical dialogue on just what our educational system does deliver to society, and what each individual state or district has an opportunity to positively impact.[28]

Example: Government Agency

So often, social responsibility is talked about through the lens of corporate responsibility, but any organization impacts society. Whether you turn a profit or not, your organization has either a positive or negative impact on society. There is a tendency in the public sector to assume that a given entity is there for the good of society because, at least in conception, that's the whole reason for having federal, state and local government entities. However, these organizations are no less off the hook for the consequences they deliver to society, as exemplified by the Department of Veterans Affairs vignette in Chapter 1. Let's consider another type of agency—the Department of Transportation.

Maintaining the Societal Infrastructure[29]

Caitlyn looked over the shoulder of her seat at their children, sound asleep in their car seats. Their vacation had been a long time coming, and they were all enjoying their time in the mile-high city of Denver and the natural beauty of the nearby mountains. She and Richard and the kids would be headed home tomorrow. They passed in the evening hours through the city landscape, headed to her sister's house. However, up ahead, an I-beam for one of the overpasses had lost the last necessary bit of concrete to hold it in place. Residents had complained for years about the concrete falling from the overpass, but nothing had been done yet. In one stroke of fateful timing, the I-beam finally gave and landed on their SUV, killing everyone inside.

The scene in the media showed a massive I-beam across the highway mangled with a big, black SUV, flashing lights all around, and a major interstate shut down with traffic backed up for miles in both directions. Within seconds, the local media was questioning the construction and the inspection processes. In the coming days, they located records of past reports on the bridge from inspectors urging fixes soon, as well as some inspections that had passed the bridge for safety. The trail led back to two key decisions, one pre-construction and one post-construction. The construction company that built the bridge had decided to save costs by using a lower grade concrete than recommended. Over time, the poor choice of concrete showed, as it started crumbling and breaking off in small pieces under the widely varying weather conditions of the climate. Nearby residents were getting chips in their windshields from small chunks of concrete falling and had registered numerous complaints. Little by little, as the small chips of concrete fell, the support for the large I-beam gave way until there simply wasn't enough concrete to hold up the I-beam.

Additionally, there were conflicting inspection reports on the construction. One report, rendered by an inspector who specialized in overpasses, called for immediate repairs to the bridge including shutting down that section entirely to rebuild it with appropriate materials. Another inspection, however, concluded that a serious failure would not happen soon because the erosion of

(continued)

Maintaining the Societal Infrastructure (continued)

> concrete was happening in such small amounts over time, and therefore this project did not rise to the level of an immediate priority. The company leaned heavily on the second report in its public defense. Regardless of what the second report said, however, the contractor had damaged its reputation, costing it millions of dollars in canceled and potential contracts (far more than the cost of quality-grade concrete), in addition to the settlement amount for a wrongful death suit. By the way they had conducted business, they demonstrated to society that money was more important than consequences to people, and as a result, society called on the terms of the social contract and ceased business with such a partner.

This is the very sort of thing that leads to reorganizations, oversight by outside agencies, and also puts companies out of business: poor decisions that demonstrate disregard for consequences communicate to society that the business would rather profit than ensure public safety. In a cynical age, we may joke that it's "human nature" to want the quick profit, and that we'll never stop it. However, it's also "human nature" to avoid those things which bring us harm. We won't put our children in faulty car seats. We won't purchase airline tickets on an airline with a string of accidents. And we actively refuse to buy vehicles made by a company that knowingly puts a dangerous product on the market. With profit motives (seemingly) out of the picture, though, the stakeholders no longer have purchasing power as a voice. What they do have, however, is their voting power— exercise through who is elected to lead and which agencies are allotted how much funding. Government agencies are directly accountable for what they do, produce and deliver to society.

While different agencies have different purposes, ultimately their purpose is to have a positive impact on one of the socially-desirable ends identified in this chapter. Whether it's safety, death rates, injuries, illness, discrimination, shelter and food, or a self-sufficient population, clearly articulated visions and missions for these entities can (and should) be revised to specifically focus on the desired societal impact that agency will have.

Example: Application in Military Organization

Finally, let's look at application in a military context before we discuss *your* organization's social contributions. To some, this sort of example seems so obvious, and to others this seems like a contradiction of terms. To military strategists and planners, however, this represents both a current known gap and a future refinement for military planning models. Desired social outcomes and ethical performance are on the minds of major military planners around the world, especially in the larger international militaries, as it is increasingly finding its way into curricula at military institutions. In this example, we begin to explore how social responsibility can be integrated into military planning models.

In this context, the old adage of winning the battle but losing the war becomes particularly relevant. Military planning that does not take social impact into consideration can accomplish victories on the battlefield—the military equivalent to an organization that successfully produces tires—but still have a larger, disastrous impact on society that in-turn impacts the military organization and its ability to function. The book started with the notion of ethics being about consequences that are "as real as it gets," and this holds especially true in military contexts. Success at a tactical level that does not lead to improved societal impact (or worse, has a negative societal impact) can actually interfere with a military organization's ability to decrease threats to national security (an assumed objective for any non-terrorist military organization). Said to the point, military planning that does not include societal planning can actually create conditions for on-going threats to security.

Like Kaufman stated about education,[30] military organizations do not operate in a vacuum, and in truth what they do and accomplish is of concern to those who pay for it, pass the legislation to support it, and rely on it to be self-sufficient. If, in the end, a given military activity does not allow citizens to live better and contribute better, it is probably not worth doing and will be condemned, and budgets will be reduced by taxpayers and legislators as well.

First, let's explore how such thinking and planning actually furthers the mission of military institutions. In an article in *USA Today*, two retired U.S. military officers (one Marine and one Navy pilot) succinctly articulate the argument and vision.[31] In their article, Zinni and Smith call for a "vibrant" strategic agenda for national security and foreign policy based on the reality that many threats to security and national interests—such as illegal immigration, terrorism, or public health and environmental problems—stem from complex social problems. For example, young people living in countries where there is high poverty and/or violence and few opportunities are "prime recruiting targets" for participating in or instigating riot, terrorism and war. They argue,

> "We cannot inoculate our nation from these threats. Instead, we must address the roots of these complex problems. Simply put, it is time to repair our relationship with the world and begin to take it to the next level—a level defined not only by our military strength, but also by the lives we save and the opportunities we create for the people of other nations...Whether it's taking the lead in increasing funding for and using innovation to expand access to potable water in the Middle East, decreasing rates of HIV/AIDS in Africa and Southeast Asia, building international partnerships to put impoverished kids in school or addressing climate change, the next administration must reframe and restructure our foreign policy and national security architecture. We must match our military might with a new commitment to investing in improving people's lives overseas."

Military power as it has been traditionally defined will not address the underlying causes of terrorism or other threats to national security so long as it is treated in isolation from the social causes that lead to the threats. But military might and military strategy conceived of in systemic terms yields a refined mission, which translates into refined operations and tactics, and on into a refined use of the resources available. Few

organizations have the resources, infrastructures, and rein-
forced lines of command at their disposal as military organizations. When these organizations begin to channel socially
desirable results through their planning and operational channels, indeed they have much to leverage and much to deliver—
to the country they protect as well as to the countries where
they have to conduct their business. This does not mean we
transform the business of the military into something else;
rather, when we recognize that military actions have social
impact and that these social situations are intertwined with the
causes of threat to security, truly strategic planning has to take
into consideration how the military will deliver desirable social
impacts. Zinni and Smith state, "Today, our 'enemies' are often
conditions—poverty, infectious disease, political instability and
corruption, global warming—which generate the biggest threats.
By addressing them in meaningful ways, we can forestall crises."

Thus, an approach that plans both for desired social successes and desired military successes will include plans for
how the underlying social circumstances in an unstable area
will be addressed. In this regard, the military infrastructure can
become a conduit for delivering a solution *set* (not just a single
solution) into an area where complex problems demand a
complex, and therefore varied, solution set. This is not entirely
new as an approach for military planning. While details of how
Mega has been applied in some organizations are not available
yet for public consumption, there are some historical examples
we can draw on. For instance, strategies in some planning
have included a focus on rebuilding or creating the ideal conditions for democracy and self-sufficiency. When these sorts of
societal-level planning objectives are not mapped out, conditions can get murky and even backfire quickly (as evidenced
most recently in Iraq). Conversely, in other places where
societal planning was incorporated into military planning, desirable conditions for stability yielded that country's or region's
stability and self-sufficiency, as well as increases to the
defending country's security. Some of the best-known examples include the Marshall Plan in postwar Europe, and compa-
rable efforts in Japan (and in South Korea after the Korean

War), which have brought generations of peace and prosperity to societies once devastated by war.

Zinni and Smith (2008) call upon the Commander in Chief and upper level planners to plan for these results in much the same way they plan for military successes. The mission has to be clearly articulated to troops, with real commitments of people and resources. In other words, we plan for desired social results in the same way we plan for desired military results.

In Moore, Ellsworth, and Kaufman, a specific example for military planning at the strategic level looked like:

> United Nations to be "at peace." All coalition force operations will be conducted in accordance with U.S. and international law, as indicated by no upheld successful prosecutions of coalition personnel in military or international courts for offenses causing loss of life, limb, and/or livelihood. There will be no loss of non-combatant civilian life attributed to coalition force operations as certified by Provincial government or United Nations monitors.[32]

This Ideal Vision-linked statement, or Mega-level objective, identifies specific types of societal impact—death, injury, and crime—and details how impact will be measured and what the specific indicators and parameters will be.

Other specific indicators of societal impact that military organizations can track include impact on mental health, such as rates of Post-Traumatic Stress Disorder and suicide rates, and environmental damage due to installations. As planners and strategists take these sorts of social impact measures into consideration, they can begin to identify the *desired* impact on a region and on society at large. And just as these considerations for positive impact should flow down into an organization to departmental levels, so these consequences should be considered by leaders on the ground making decisions about specific tactics and whether those tactics have a negative impact at the global level.

Additional Examples:

There are numerous examples of actual organizations applying this form of social responsibility, or Mega Planning, in their strategic planning. These cases include the Vocational Rehabilitation Program at Florida Division of Blind Services, Refinor gas production and distribution company in Argentina, the State of Ohio's Workforce Development program, start-up planning that integrates social responsibility, and applications for Civil Society Organizations (CSOs) with an example from Asociación Conciencia in Argentina. The collection also represents examples from around the globe, including the United States, Australia, Mexico and Argentina.[33]

Socially Desirable Ends: Your Organization's Deliverables

We examined a few other cases in Chapter 1 that highlighted how different organizations impact social measures—such as Topps Meat and their impact on disease (making people sick with contaminated beef products), and suicide rates among veterans. Throughout the book, I've also referenced examples where government agencies impact shelter, starvation and/or malnutrition, child abuse, or discrimination. So now, in light of these examples and a new understanding of how your organization contributes to society, it's time for you to determine what part of the whole your organization is responsible for. These are the deliverables of your social contract with society.

Think back through these examples, or even re-read them as necessary. Review how these organizations ended up impacting society. It can be hard to pull back the film over our eyes when it comes to realizing our social impact, so these examples should hopefully help you think of results of your organization. Use the following as guiding questions:

- Is there something about the way that we do business that increases bias, whether intended or not? (For example, do your policies or technical infrastructure exclude some individuals unnecessarily?)

- Do we produce a product that, if not designed or produced well, could lead to injury, illness, accidents, war, terrorism, or riot, environmental damage, pollution, or crime?

- Are individuals more or less self-sufficient as a result of what we do (or do we assume they are or want them to be)?

- Is there something in our current work environment that leads to increased substance abuse, illness, depression, accidents, or other undesirable effects?

- Is it really supposed to be our business to provide shelter or reduce child abuse, partner/spousal abuse, drug addiction, disease, poverty, war, or crimes against people or property?

Now, with other leaders in your organization or industry or even within your department, discuss the following and place checkmarks by each socially-responsible end to determine which ones you impact directly, indirectly, and not at all. You should have at least one check mark in each category.

Basic Ideal Vision Elements—There will be no loss of life or elimination of the survival of any species required for human survival. There will be no reductions in levels of self-sufficiency, quality of life, livelihood, or loss of property from any source, including:	My Organization Makes a Contribution...		
	Directly	**Indirectly**	**None**
War and/or riot and/or terrorism			
Shelter			
Unintended human-caused changes to the environment, including permanent destruction of the environment and/or rendering it non-renewable.			
Murder, rape, or crimes of violence, robbery, or destruction to property			
Substance abuse			
Disease			
Pollution			
Starvation and/or malnutrition			
Child abuse			
Partner/spouse/elder abuse			
Accidents, including transportation, home, and business/workplace			
Discrimination based on irrelevant variables, including color, race, creed, sex, religion, national origin, age, and location			
Poverty will not exist, and every woman and man will earn at least as much as it costs him or her to live unless he or she is progressing toward being self-sufficient and self-reliant			
No adult will be under the care, custody, or control of another person, agency, or substance. All adult citizens will be self-sufficient and self-reliant as minimally indicated by their consumption being equal to or less than their production			

Used with permission from Kaufman, 2006a

These are the socially-desirable ends your organization impacts. In the next chapter, we'll write organizational objects (across levels of an organization) based on these socially-desirable results. The things your organization does, produces, and delivers are means to these ends. By planning, designing, producing and acting towards these ends, your organization is no longer part of a strategically-tragic tradition. Instead, you start to become a part of the solution, not part of the problem.

Add your agreed-upon checklist of the above elements to the initial social contract statement. You have just identified your deliverables. By now, you have a commitment to the social contract and identified contract deliverables.

At this point, we have to add the layer of complexity known as strategic partnerships.

Ethical Bedfellows: Whom You Work with to Achieve Desired Ends

The social responsibility of other entities whom you do business or partner with is just as critical as what your organization specifically commits to. Let's recall the marbles metaphor—your partners are marbles with which you are purposefully interconnected by choice, so what they do, produce and deliver impacts you. Companies that otherwise maintain fairly clean records for themselves can be caught unaware, and suffer negative consequences, when a "strategic" partner doesn't hold equally high standards. These partnerships are a critical part of the ends you deliver, since you've chosen them (in theory) because you believe they will help you attain desired ends. Thus, we'll address your strategic partnerships here in this chapter. You have to make sure your whole team is committed to these same socially-desirable ends—both your internal team and your external team.

Let's examine partnerships in context of a case study.

The CEO of Mattell, Inc. insisted Tuesday that his company has "rigorous standards" and apologized as the company was forced to recall millions of toys for the second time in two weeks.

The Serious Business of Play[34]

"The company has ordered that all products be pulled off retail shelves," said Nancy Nord, acting chairman of The U.S. Consumer Product Safety Commission.

Parents were suddenly faced with having to sift through the piles of toys in their kids' rooms to find products and tiny codes on the bottom to see which ones should be thrown out. Those toys, it turned out, could cause sickness or death.

In late 2007, Mattel recalled 9 million more toys only days after Fisher Price (of which Mattel is the parent company) recalled 1.5 million toys, pulling products off store shelves. It turned out that business partners in China weren't producing at "rigorous standards"—toys manufactured in China were found to contain lead, and some contained small magnets that could easily come off toys. That lead could poison children if they ingested parts or paint off the toys containing lead, and the magnets posed a clear choking hazard. In total, 10.5 million toys in the U.S. and 11 million world-wide were recalled.

Mattel's Chief Executive Officer, Bob Eckert, appeared to understand, at least outwardly, that this sort of event breaks the biggest contract—the contract with society. Parents trust that the company will deliver safe Products their children can play with. When that sort of trust is broken, the social contract is broken. And it can be very hard to get the customer back.

Eckert apologized and asserted that Mattel has a long safety record that makes it a trusted name. However, one incident can ruin an otherwise unblemished record—especially when it is the health and safety of children that have been put at risk. Mattel is still in the throes of regaining public trust. Their first step—a sweeping recall—has a track record for being a good first step in regaining public trust. It's an act of ownership, of taking responsibility for the problem. However, there are many steps ahead—to include how the company improves its quality assurance procedures to avoid having to recall any toys ever again *and* how it identifies desirable partners for accomplishing that end, as well as quality toys that are delivered to market.

Increasingly, as companies and the marketplace become global in scope and structure, leaders face the challenge of identifying partners around the globe that meet the same level of standards as the parent company claims to uphold. Your partners have to be committed to the same desirable societal outcomes as your organization. Business partners may manufacture parts, provide a particular service, transport your goods, or build a part of your internal infrastructure such as the information technology backbone. Social responsibility in the practices of potential partners has become a critical criterion for selection. In the past, this criterion (if even acknowledged) may have been disregarded because, it was argued, organizations could not possibly "police" other organizations on their business practices. Today, however, as the Mattel incident demonstrates, those with whom you do business reflect upon your own organization and the public's perception of how good a job you're doing upholding your contract with society. Companies like Starbucks and Celestial Seasonings, who have to conduct business with coffee or tea growers around the world, have begun to institute high review standards to determine desirable partners both for Products and for social responsibility.

In the act of choosing certain business partners, a business communicates what value it chooses to add to society. That choice, and its resulting consequences, can be very costly if socially responsible criteria are ignored, as Mattel has discovered.

Tool: Evaluating Potential Business Partners

Business partners are selected based on a set of criteria, so the application of strict criteria and close scrutiny of potential partners is nothing new. Given that the selection process already involves a process of scrutiny, adding social responsibility to the criteria set does not add any additional workload or invasive practices into the review and selection process.

The following quick evaluation tool can be integrated into a partner selection process to ensure your company or organization does business with desirable partners instead of partners who will harm your financial bottom line by harming your social bottom line.

Potential Partner Pledge

Questions Organizations Must Ask about Potential Partners	Do You Commit:	
	Yes	No
Does this potential partner commit to deliver products, services, or educational contributions that add value for your externals AND society? (Mega/Outcomes)		
Does this potential partner commit to deliver products, services, or educational contributions that have the quality required by other external partners? (Macro/Outputs)		
Does this potential partner commit to internal results that have the quality required by your internal partners? (Micro/Products)		
Does this potential partner commit to have efficient internal products, programs, projects, and activities? (Processes)		
Does this potential partner commit to create and ensure the quality and appropriateness of the human, capital, and physical resources available? (Inputs)		
Does this potential partner commit to deliver: a. Products, activities, methods, and procedures that have positive value and worth? b. The results and accomplishments defined by our objectives?		
Evaluation/Continuous Improvement		

(Adapted, with permission, from Kaufman, 2000, 2006a)

In addition to the questions provided above, it is most effective to get specific in your criteria based on the nature of the partnership and what outcomes or results will be delivered by that partner. For example, you could specify:

- Does this potential business partner commit to deliver toys that will not result in the death or sickness of a single child due to any unsafe practices or faulty parts, as measured by the number of lawsuits, or any voluntary or mandatory recalls?

Examples for other industries might include:

- Does this potential business partner commit to the delivery of protective combat gear that will reduce death and injury, including traumatic brain injury, for all troops in theater?

- Does this potential partner commit to quality assurance procedures that yield no more than 0.001% defective parts for our airplanes and which will never result in a fatal crash?

- Does this potential partner commit to deliver safe ice, water, and/or basic foods to victims of natural disaster within 24 hours of the end of the event, and distribute that basic food and water to victims to ensure 100% of those affected receive food and water within 24 hours and will not die or become permanently disabled from contamination, dehydration, or starvation?

Just as your business or organizational partners help your organization create the products and services you want to deliver to the market with the desired results (usually increased profit), so they are your same partners in the outcomes you deliver. They are your partners in the social contract, not just in production. Their commitment to positive social outcomes (or lack thereof) will reflect on your organization, and on your bottom line. Integrating this criterion into your partnership selection process will ensure that even in whom you do business with (not just how you do it), you keep a focus on the desired outcomes, products and results of your organization.

Otherwise, the cost of doing business with that particular partner may be more than you care to afford, and the financial and social impact of that decision won't be evident until you're standing in front of a bank of microphones and reporters apologizing to parents around the world.

Articulating the Whole Contract: Adding Your Deliverables and Your Partners in Those Deliverables

In the previous chapter, we defined social responsibility as a strategic business plan and highlighted the social contract every organization manages. You started that contract by:

1) Acknowledging your organization's contract with society, and

2) Committing to add measurable value to society.

In this chapter, we outlined further terms of this contract by:

3) Identifying measurable societal outcomes that your organization contributes to, and

4) Setting clear standards for any partners with whom you do business to accomplish these desired outcomes and outputs.

Now, let's turn that commitment and those deliverables into a strategic course of action. In the next chapter, you will:

5) Articulate measurable organizational objectives to be used for strategic planning that are tied to desirable societal outcomes, and

6) Align those desirable outcomes down into the processes, tasks and inputs of your organization.

The table below provides the answers to the Ends and Means Checklist on page 38

Item	Ends	Means
Train our staff on diversity		✓
Graduation	✓	
Assessing needs		✓
Reorganization		✓
Policies on workplace diversity		✓
Positive credit rating	✓	
Death/injury	✓	
Increased communication between IT and other departments		✓
Reduce welfare funding		✓
Increased attention to student needs		✓
Benchmarking		✓
Increase prison funding		✓
Decrease class size		✓
Performance or merit-based pay increases		✓
Learning problem solving		✓

Endnotes

1. Mager, 1997—part of the Mager "six pack"

2. Watkins, 2007

3. Kaufman, 2000, 2006

4. Moore, Ellsworth & Kaufman, 2008

5. Kaufman, 2000, 2006

6. Oakley-Browne, 2007; McClelland, 1961

7. Ibid, p.5

8. As well as validating why we should get there…based on data from a valid needs assessment.

9. McDonough, 2006

10. Berenbeim, 1987; Dean, 1993

11. Letter from Thomas Jefferson to James Madison, Paris, September 6, 1789. For the full text, see p. 375 of Foley's *The Jeffersonian Cyclopedia*.

12. Kaufman, 2000; Kaufman, in press; Guerra-Lopez, 2005; Kaufman & Watkins, 1999; also cite 2005 PIQ issue

13. Kaufman, 2000, p.94

14. Moore, 2005; also in the PIQ/2005 Special Issue

15. Kaufman, 2000

16. Kaufman, 2000, 2006

17. In their 2006 article in Harvard Business Review, Porter and Kramer articulate many of the same practical approaches to truly strategic social responsibility advanced in this book. In particular, most authors on this topic will note that your organization isn't responsible for everything…the strategic planning process means you identify precisely what contribution you do make, and then plan to have a positive impact on that.

18. This specific example comes from the one-page brief that was added to their 2006 article, "Strategy & Society" published in *Harvard Business Review*. The original article itself will not include that example or the one-page summary, but the purchasable copy through *Harvard Business Review* online does:

http://harvardbusinessonline.hbsp.harvard.edu/b01/en/common/it em_detail.jhtml?id=R0612D&_requestid=46501. I like how this one example so succinctly captures how truly strategic planning benefits society, which then in turn benefits your organization.

19. Hansen, C. (2007). Hot iPods: Is there a way to stop thieves cold? A Dateline hidden camera investigation. http://www.msnbc. msn.com/id/20078671/ Accessed August 6, 2007.

20. The patent was filed on December 20, 2005, US Patent Application 0070138999.

21. Rogers, E. (2003). *Diffusion of innovations* (5th ed). New York: Free Press.

22. Personal Communications, James Groves, Asst. Dean of Research and Outreach, University of Virginia School of Engineering and Applied Sciences

23. Stolovich & Keeps, 1999; Villachica & Stone, 1999; there are other types of systemic barriers to ideal performance, but here we look at consequences

24. Deming, 1972, 1982, 1986; Juran, 1988

25. (Kaufman, 1996, p. 112, reprinted from 1977)

26. Kaufman, Watkins & Guerra, 2002

27. 2005—from PIQ issue

28. Chow, 2008; Chow, Whitlock & Moore, 2007

29. This narrative is based on actual events in Denver, Colorado. On May 15, 2004, a girder supporting an overpass over the major interstate of I-70 in the Denver metro area fell, killing a family of three inside an SUV. The actual events were reported by KMGH, the ABC affiliate in Denver.

30. 1996—Kaufman's chapter in Ely's collection Classics

31. March 27, 2008—link if possible

32. 2008—Moore, Ellsworth, Kaufman

33. In the 2005 issue of *Performance Improvement Quarterly* (volume 18, number 3)

34. An archived version of this report can be found on CNN— http://www.cnn.com/2007/US/08/14/recall/index.html.

Chapter 3
Nailing Mud: Socially Responsible Strategic Planning

"....It's no longer acceptable for us to say this isn't part of our plan. . .because it's part of our de facto *plan. It's the thing that's happening because we have no other plan."*

William McDonough[1]

Undesirable societal results happen because we simply don't plan for them to be otherwise. So let's build that other plan—the one in which negative impacts on society aren't *de facto* results.

The first step is defining desired ends. In the previous chapter, we outlined different socially desirable ends and identified which ones you impact. Every organization impacts one or some of those ends, and together we impact them all. All organizations are subsystems of our shared system of society. With those ends in mind, we'll now build a plan towards those desired ends.

Objectives offer your organization a chance to *plan* for desired effects, and align those plans within an organization. Most strategic planning focuses on desired organizational outcomes—increased sales, increased graduation, improved service, etc.

Social responsibility works precisely the same way: setting effective objectives that target the societal level offers the organization a chance to plan for desired effects. By not including these, unintended societal impact becomes part of the de facto plan. By including these, however, and starting from the level of desired societal outcomes rather than organizational outcomes, you can plan towards social responsibility and the longevity that perspective brings.

There are three major levels of planning for any organization. Every single level, or layer, of planning has to be addressed. When these are addressed collectively, then you achieve alignment from what you want to deliver down into the bowels of your organization.

Specifically, the three levels of planning, or consequences are Mega, Macro and Micro[2]—and the corresponding objectives must be both well-articulated *and aligned* across all three (see The Organizational Elements table below). The quality (or lack thereof, or even total absence) of these objectives will show up in how your organization performs—both in terms of productivity/profit as well as societal impact. The quality of Micro-level objectives, for instance, will show up in the performance of individuals and small groups within your organization... and also in the quality—defined as fitness for use—of the products your organization delivers.

Organizational Element	Level of Planning and Focus	Brief Description
Outcomes	Mega	Results and their consequences for external clients and society
Outputs	Macro	The results an organization can or does deliver outside of itself
Products	Micro	The building-block results that are produced within the organization
Processes	Process	The ways, means, activities, procedures, and methods used internally
Inputs	Input	The human, physical, and financial resources the organization can or does use

From Kaufman, R. (2000, 2006a)

So, as you engage in strategic planning, truly strategic planning starts at what Kaufman calls the Mega level: society. What are your organization's desired results and their consequences for external clients and society? Do you want the public to pass over bridges and other city infrastructures to reach their destinations safely (safety is the Mega level measure)? Do you want prisoners who are released from your facilities to be rehabilitated to the point they never commit another crime again (or better yet, work with other organizations to ensure nobody comes to you in the first place)? Do you want your graduates to obtain jobs that make them self-sufficient and/or be active in building opportunities that bring stability and increased self-sufficiency or environmental benefits to the local economy?

Peter Orszag, Director of the White House Office of Management and Budget for the Obama administration, began to differentiate between these levels of results as he talked about designing towards a more "effective" and efficient health care system. In an interview with NPR, he stated,

> "Estimates suggest that as much as $700 billion a year in health care costs do not improve health outcomes. It occurs because we pay for more care rather than better care. We 'need' to be moving towards a system in which doctors and hospitals have incentives to provide the care that makes you better, rather than the care that just results in more tests and more days in [the] hospital."[3]

Data shows (remember from Chapter 1—"if you care, get the facts") that just because some hospitals may do more, patients in those hospitals don't necessarily exhibit a higher level of desired outcomes—i.e., better health. We would expect that as hospitals do more, that patient health would increase. This is an excellent case in point of the difference between process (doing) and results (outcomes). Orszag also speaks right to the heart of the distinction between different levels of objectives that are necessary. An organization could deliver great Micro or Macro results (such as more tests or more time in care), but still not deliver desirable outcomes. In this case, the desired outcome is clear: better health. And yet, "doing more" isn't translating into better health. To yield better health, a Mega-level outcome, a system transformation is in order. That entails starting with the true desired outcome (better health, or higher employment or decreased abuse—whatever your organization is in the business of) and then aligning that ultimate outcome strategically down through the very Macro and Micro level objectives of your organization, on into your processes and inputs.

Strategic planning starts at the level of what results (not what products) you deliver to external clients and society—the Mega level. Then, you plan what results your organization will deliver outside itself—the Macro level. This level of results includes any increased sales, timeliness, increased efficiency or ease of use, graduation rates, number of cases handled and resolved, and so forth. The most common objectives are written at the Macro level, when a company states it wants to be the leading organization in what it delivers (e.g., the leading producer of greeting cards or the leading engineering program in the United States). And then finally, you plan for the quality of products, as when a company sets objectives around fewer defective parts or more paper goods produced from recycled and recyclable materials. Those desired objectives then align downward into the critical processes for the organization to accomplish those ends and the necessary resources the organization can use to get there.

Aligning Societal Level Objectives Down Into Your Organization

Let's look at some detailed examples of good objectives at the Mega, Macro and Micro levels, and then examine how to align and why alignment is so important. These examples span across settings to demonstrate how these sorts of objectives can be developed in any environment. The first three examples are used with permission from an article on writing useful objectives by Moore, Ellsworth & Kaufman.[4]

A Mega-Level Example Objective

Among the new expectations for organizations is a growing demand from their customers or constituents for them to be socially responsive and responsible. *Mega*-level objectives represent the planner's tools for achieving these expectations. An example provided earlier—a military example—shows how an entity can clearly articulate Mega-level objectives:

> By the conclusion of Ramadan, non-combatant civilians residing in the Province will suffer no greater rates of violent death or injury than those seen from baseline crime rates in surrounding countries deemed by the United Nations to be "at peace." All coalition force operations will be conducted in accordance with U.S. and international law, as indicated by no upheld successful prosecutions of coalition personnel in military or international courts for offenses causing loss of life, limb, and/or livelihood. There will be no loss of non-combatant civilian life attributed to coalition force operations as certified by Provincial government or United Nations monitors.

Examples of Mega-level outcomes are measured based on the set of 13 societal results covered in chapter 2. These include such indicators as health and well-being, consequences of pollution, accidents, discrimination, poverty, substance abuse, disease, shelter, war and/or riot, harm to environment, starvation (or malnutrition), child abuse, partner/spousal abuse, and self-sufficiency. Notice how, in this military example, desirable societal results are stated clearly and focus on measurable outcomes. In addition, the objective details precisely what will be measured and by whom or by what criteria. It establishes a very clear standard for what the desired social impact of the military in that region will be. There are many additional examples across other industries provided at the end of this chapter.

A Macro-Level Example Objective

The quality of the second level of objectives, *Macro*-level objectives, will appear in the outputs of your organization. Outputs are the things an organization can or does deliver outside itself (*e.g.,* manufactured automobiles, educated graduates, defeated adversaries)—not to be confused with the *actual effects* created by delivery of those things. A well-defined output is a clear definition of what your organization puts out into the surrounding marketplace or environment. For example, an output can be "provide timely aid to victims of natural disaster" (poorly-defined). . .or alternatively (a government example):

> After October of this year, at least 99% of all families rendered homeless by any natural disaster will receive adequate emergency shelter within 48 hours after the disaster event ends, where inadequacy is indicated by number of substantiated complaints (including health and nutrition-related consequences) that shelter did not protect occupants from the elements and was unsafe when provided.

Traditional planning usually originates at Macro-level— often mislabeled "strategic"—planning. While this is a critical part of the process, effective planning must begin at the Mega level.

A Micro-Level Example Objective

Objectives at this level cascade from well-developed Mega and Macro objectives. A well-developed objective at the *Micro*-level might state (a corporate example):

> Cellular telephones and bundled accessories delivered to final assembly and shipping will meet all quality acceptance standards and criteria, as indicated by sign-off of the quality inspector on each shift and no greater than 0.2% rejects from the quality assurance test laboratory.

Such a clearly-defined objective at the Micro level articulates precisely what the target is and how you'll know when you have achieved it. It does not presuppose the means, methods, approaches and activities to achieve the objective; instead, it clearly focuses on ends and not means. However, an objective at this level does not specify what the evidence should be that the organization as a whole is meeting its purposes (Macro level) or adding value for its external clients and society (Mega level).

Depending on how well defined your organization's objectives are at the Mega, Macro and Micro levels, the activities of your organization and the individuals within will yield either weeds or fruit. This is true no matter your context, be it in the public or private sector, profit-driven or not-for-profit. Gearing your organization's tasks, products, outputs and outcomes towards useful, productive "fruit" requires close attention to alignment of objectives across levels, and to how quality objectives are constructed in the first place.

Separating the Good from the Bad, the Useful from the Non-useful. Just as we separated ends from means, it's good to make sure we can distinguish between clear, well-defined objectives and poorly-defined objectives. Just having an objective is not good enough. Objectives can vary in quality, and different objectives can yield very different results. Objectives are at the core of defining how your organization will perform. Thus, it's important to start by separating the wheat from the chaff.

Many "strategic" plans or assessment plans for organizations or departments start with a statement of desired "outcomes." (Outcomes are actually the results you deliver at the societal level, not within your organization, and many organizations have poor clarification between these levels. So we'll clarify that in a bit.) Those "outcomes" are really imposters for strategic planning, often looking something like the following:

- Develop diversity training for our staff

- Increase the number of hours of tutoring provided to our students

- Increase the number of sales to customers in the Southern California region

- Improve customer service

- Decrease the number of defects coming off the manufacturing lines

- Foster increased communication between faculty and students on campus using social networking technologies

- Become the leading producer of organic groceries in the world

And so on.

We're so used to so-called "objectives" or "goals" or "mission statements" that look like these that it's probably hard to see why these are poorly developed objectives that mix means and ends. In fact, a few in there might actually be looking pretty good. But they're not. One is a Micro level objective, but that's a low layer in your organization—not a higher-level strategic objective. And it's not a very good objective because it lacks clear definition. The rest are means to accomplishing ends.

Often, means are pre-selected and stated right in the objective. Objectives are about the destination, not the way you'll get there. In the examples above, five of the seven "objectives" are actually means to ends. Review those and ask yourself, "Is this is a result or a way to achieve a result?" In the table on the next page, indicate whether you think the objective statement is a Means or an End based on what we've covered so far. Answers are on pages 94–95.

Objective Statement	Means or End
Develop diversity training for our staff	
Increase the number of hours of tutoring provided to our students	
Increase the number of sales to customers in the Southern California region	
Improve customer service	
Decrease the number of defects coming off the manufacturing lines	
Foster increased communication between faculty and students on campus using social networking technologies	
Become the leading producer of organic groceries in the world	

How did you do? Here are the answers with an explanation for each.

Objective Statement	Means or End
Develop diversity training for our staff	**Means**—training is always a means to an end; what is the diversity training supposed to accomplish? How will they know if it's effective? The answers to those questions would actually drive how the training is developed (or if it's even a training issue at all).
Increase the number of hours of tutoring provided to our students	**Means**—even though the increase in hours could be measured, that doesn't mean it's a meaningful number; what is the tutoring supposed to result in—only an increase in hours? Or an increase in students' grades? An actual end here would be increasing student grades (in a given course or on a topic, for example). Tutoring might be the means for accomplishing that objective.
Increase the number of sales to customers in the Southern California region	**End**—yes, sales are a measurable end. However, the point of this book is that strategic planning doesn't stop here. This is a lower-order end (Macro level—we'll look at that in a bit). You could achieve increased sales in a region but still miss other targets. You might sell more in Southern California, but if the product is defective or leads to safety issues, you've poorly planned for larger strategic successes.
Improve customer service	**Means**—besides being vague, this statement is a means for accomplishing an end. Because this is so generic, it's hard to know just what would be improved, much less what strategy or action would achieve the desired result; most likely, this office wants to see a decrease in the number of customer complaints and/or an increase in customer compliments.

Decrease the number of defects coming off the manufacturing lines	**End**—this statement is actually an end statement; with this end clearly defined, the management can determine what strategy will best help them accomplish this end. They might want to conduct a needs assessment to diagnose precisely what the problem is and then select a strategy based on the needs assessment; however, this objective is at a Micro level.
Foster increased communication between faculty and students on campus using social networking technologies	**Means**—many a strategic planning document contains "objectives" that look like this one—very nice words that don't mean much. One question to ask is "how will you know when you've arrived"—if you can't answer that question, it's a poorly-defined objective.
Become the leading producer of organic groceries in the world	**End**—while this is an end, it is a poorly-articulated objective. It doesn't include any clear measures or indicators for success, any criteria or timeframes. This is a Macro-level objective.

A job aid for separating out good objectives from bad objectives is included in Appendix B (used with permission from Moore, Ellsworth and Kaufman).[5]

Expanded Examples of Socially Responsible Strategic Planning Across Different Types of Organization. In this section, we are going to look at detailed examples of Mega, Macro and Micro objectives for different types of organizations. While your organization may not look exactly like these or may identify other gaps to address, these should serve as clear road maps for what socially responsible strategic planning really does and can look like.

We start with several examples that articulate objectives at the Mega, Macro and Micro level that are aligned. We finish with one example where many more details are fleshed out to demonstrate how Mega is identified and then aligned down into the processes and inputs of an organization.

Take these, use these, and adapt these as templates to guide your organization on its path to desired performance. By no means are these meant to imply the details herein are what an organization should do, but instead these are examples of how you clearly define objectives at every level, starting with a Mega-level objective and aligning it downward into the bowels of your organization. It should also be noted that there does tend to be a branching and blossoming effect when the full planning process is employed (i.e., for every one Macro objective there are several Micro objectives to support it.) Every possible branch is not captured in these examples.

Example Organization: Department of Health and Human Services	
Mega	There will be no death of or serious permanent injuries to children as the result of physical abuse, to include abuse by neglect of any sort among cases reported to the Department of Health and Human Services subsequent to the date the case is reported.
Macro	No child with immediate evidence of physical abuse or neglect shall be left in the residence under review but shall instead be removed to an alternate, safe location by the time the first DHS employee on scene is leaving the scene.
Micro	There will be no instances of failed follow-up with the children and associated adults involved in reported cases (24 hours initial review, 5 days for full review), except when inclement weather that has resulted in closure of the DHS impedes the travel of a DHS employee. All primary caregivers for the child will have a thorough criminal background check conducted on them by the end of the full five-day review process.

(continued)

Department of Health and Human Services (concluded)

Processes	*24-hour initial review*—home is visited by a DHS employee, photos and videos are used to obtain immediate documentation, and every single associated adult with any sort of influence/presence in the child's life has been located and primary suspects interviewed.
	Criminal background investigations—All primary adults associated with the child will be investigated within a 48-hour time period, to include registered sex offender lists, local police records, and federal databases.
	Five-day review—100% of all reported cases will go through a thorough review within 5 days, wherein the child will receive a thorough examination from a licensed, experienced professional and all adults who have contact with the child will have been thoroughly interviewed and criminal histories reviewed.
	Removal of child—Locations that have a perfect track record for safety will be identified in advance. The child will be transported with a DHS official in a safe vehicle and will reside at the safe location.

This next example comes courtesy of James Ellsworth, personal communication (2009) as a follow-on to the Moore, Ellsworth & Kaufman (2008) article.

This objective has been written so it would apply equally to the starvation & malnutrition and disease dimensions of Mega in *either* a post-hostilities reconstruction *or* a natural disaster recovery scenario. To best illustrate alignment, *all* the Macro-level objectives underlying the Mega objective are provided, but to prevent the example from mushrooming, only the Micro-level objectives for the *first* Macro-level objective are detailed.

Example Organization: Military

Mega	By the end of the next growing season, coalition forces, in partnership with the host nation government and such non-governmental organizations as it may accredit, will (as certified by the United Nations monitors) have re-established self-sufficient, sustainable agriculture, water availability, and public health throughout the region, such that there is no loss of life or long-term productivity due to starvation, malnutrition, or disease.
Macro	Within 30 days of commencement of operations, coalition forces will (as certified by United Nations monitors) have established reliable deliveries of food, water, and medical supplies to all populated areas in the affected region. Within 60 days of commencement of operations, coalition forces will (as certified by United Nations monitors) have begun equipping and training host nation government and private sector organizations in preparation for returning the operational lead to civil authority. Within 90 days of commencement of operations, coalition forces will (as certified by United Nations monitors) have neutralized all violent threats to the integrity or timeliness of such deliveries. Within 120 days of commencement of operations, coalition forces will (as certified by United Nations monitors) have successfully restored host nation government control over agriculture, water, and public health, providing consultation and surge capacity as requested by civil authority. By the end of the next growing season, coalition forces will have redeployed from the region and removed their ecological footprint.
Micro	Each Reconstruction Team establishes terminus points for deliveries in its Area of Operations (AO) as follows: one per village or tribal area under 1,000 population; one per (roughly) 10,000 population in urban areas, with social homogeneity of serviced population as overriding factor.

(continued)

Military (continued)

	Each Reconstruction Team executes minimum of one delivery per week to each terminus point in its AO, fully meeting basic nutritional and medical requirements of the serviced population. Each Reconstruction Team ensures that no shipments in its AO are intercepted/diverted or lost to negligence. Each Reconstruction Team achieves at least a 50% reduction in average rates of pilferage/shrinkage per shipment when compared to prevailing host nation government/commercial rates prior to intervention. Each Reconstruction Team provides security at terminus points in its AO, successfully ensuring equitable and unconditional distribution of aid to its intended recipients.
Processes (what you do to arrive at your Mega, Macro, and Micro objectives)	*Diplomatic*—Ambassador and Joint/Coalition Force Commander negotiate timelines, scope, and terms of assistance with host nation government, coalition partner governments, and international or non-governmental organizations before commencement of operations. *Information*—Before and throughout the operation, Public Affairs and Psychological Operations elements publicize coalition force nutritional & public health assistance, emphasizing humanitarian intent, empowerment of the host nation & its sovereignty, and plans for full withdrawal when situation stabilized (while ensuring operational security of aid distribution is not compromised). *Military*—Coalition forces provide security for civilian population and host nation government and private sector organizations until host nation forces are consistently able to do so, and for coalition forces throughout the operation. Coalition forces provide logistical and medical capacity and supply to meet basic nutritional and medical requirements of the population until civil authority is restored.

(continued)

Military (concluded)

Economic—Agriculture, Commerce, and State Department, and Health & Human Services elements in coalition forces marshal nutritional, agricultural, and public health expertise, materiel, and foreign aid to rebuild & improve sustainable capacity in host nation government and private sector.

Finance—Commerce and Treasury elements in coalition forces identify and interdict criminal, insurgent, or terrorist funding streams and rebuild & improve host nation and private sector banking systems and accountability processes.

Intelligence—Coalition intelligence elements identify key interest groups and agendas and assess their likely influence on provision of nutritional and public health objectives of the operation. Intelligence elements identify, assess, and track threats to the integrity or timeliness of aid deliveries.

Legal—Under direction of Ambassador, Justice and Civil Affairs elements in coalition forces work with host nation authorities to negotiate Rules of Engagement (ROE), and with host nation authorities and intergovernmental organizations as appropriate to re-establish Rule of Law and make any adjustments to host nation legal frameworks necessary to facilitate aid deliveries and re-establishment of sustainable capacities in agriculture, water resources, and public health services.

Example Organization: Educational Institution
Mega There will be an increase in self-sufficiency and quality of life in the region as indicated by increased employment rates, increased rates of job creation, and increased indicators of economic stability in both rural and urban areas of the state. There will be no damage to the environment as a result of products or processes created by our students, as indicated by substantiated reports and evidence of loss of natural resources or damage to surrounding ecosystems.
Macro We will graduate at least 20% more students a year as part of our program, all of which should come from rural or other traditionally underrepresented populations in the engineering workforce. 90% of students who enter the program will complete the program, in a timely fashion, and find employment in a related job within three months of completion, as indicated by post-graduation/alumni data. Employers will consistently rate our graduates as among the best and express a preference for hiring our graduates over those from other regional programs, as indicated by employer surveys and other national comparisons of program performance.
Micro All students will receive timely one-on-one advising from a full-time faculty member, based on student reports and advising faculty documentation, which leads to academic decisions. All students will demonstrate an understanding of societal impact in their engineering designs as indicated by their performance on a final design project in which they clearly articulate the potential impact of their designs and what modifications or adaptations they made to provide a positive societal impact, as measured by a rubric. 90% of students will demonstrate good to excellent (B to A) levels of learning in at least 95% of their classes, as evidenced by their performance on in-class exams or projects and end-of-degree comprehensive exams.

(continued)

Educational Institution (concluded)

Processes	Work with partner companies to create employment opportunities for students; plan and provide employment days to connect students with potential employers. Connect every student with their primary advisor upon acceptance to program; track contacts from faculty reports via an electronic assessment program.

Example Organization: For-Profit, Manufacturing	
Mega	There will be no loss of life or serious injury due to defective parts (whether new parts off the assembly line or parts that have been in operation for many years) as measured by documented incidents, lawsuits (whether contested or settled), or recalls of products. There will be no damage to the environment that results from our manufacturing or delivery processes or from the disposal or removal of our products.
Macro	All deliveries will be on time and meet customer requirements, as indicated by customer complaints, returns, and pre-processed orders.
Micro	Cellular telephones and bundled accessories delivered to final assembly and shipping will meet all quality acceptance standards and criteria, as indicated by sign-off of the quality inspector on each shift and no greater than 0.2% rejects from the quality assurance test laboratory.

Example Organization: For-Profit, Services

Mega	There will be no serious illness or death due to consumption of our product, as indicated by death rates or illnesses traced back to our facility (whether traced through internal investigations or external investigations). Our product line will lead to increased health conditions for customers as indicated both by (a) external approvals from agencies such as the AHA (American Heart Association) and (b) double-blind studies conducted by third-party entities.[6]
Macro	All products will be delivered on time and meet customer requirements, as indicated by customer complaints, returns, and pre-processed orders. The customer base for our product line will expand from the western US region to at least two other regions of the U.S., with a stable increase of sales to at least 25% more in those two regions by year's end.
Micro	All food and beverages served to customers will meet quality acceptance standards from delivery of products to the site through delivery of products at time of service as indicated by (a) a sign-off on quality inspection on each shift and (b) a level no greater than 0.01% of reported instances of illness resulting from poor quality foods or beverages in any given year.

A footnote on these examples—by no means are these intended to convey the message that if you are the sort of organization identified that this is exactly what your objectives should look like. Effective objectives are derived specifically from the needs, or gaps, that your organization addresses. Those are identified through a quality needs assessment process. Once those gaps are effectively identified and desired ends are stated, you can articulate an objective. These are guides or templates on what quality objectives look like for each level in different types of organizations.

Articulating Measurable Objectives
and Aligning Objectives with
Processes, Inputs, and Tasks

Yes, we have reached the portion of our program where you just have to roll up your sleeves and get to work. Because each organization is different, the final articulation of these objectives will look different. The critical aspect is that they are measurable, so you know when you have arrived.[7] The preceding examples should serve as guides depending on what type of organization you are in. The following is a job aid to assist you in keeping your societal deliverables in front of you and planning strategically then aligning that planning downward.

Our organization: _____
Societal impacts we have committed to: (State the measures from the 13 Outcomes in Chapter 2 you directly impact)
Mega
Macro
Micro

(continued)

Processes (what you do to arrive at your Mega, Macro, and Micro objectives)

Tasks (what functions employees carry out to support processes)

Inputs (what resources are necessary to complete the tasks)

Articulating the Whole Contract:
Adding Clearly-Defined Objectives
Aligned along Mega, Macro, and Micro

In the previous chapters, we defined social responsibility as a strategic business plan and highlighted the social contract every organization manages. You started that contract by:

1) Acknowledging your organization's contract with society, and

2) Committing to add value to society.

In Chapter 2, we outlined further terms of this contract by:

3) Identifying measurable societal outcomes that your organization contributes to, and

4) Setting clear standards for any partners with whom you do business to accomplish these desired outcomes and outputs.

Now, we have fleshed out the details of this contract by:

5) Articulating measurable organizational objectives to be used for strategic planning that are tied to desirable societal outcomes, and

6) Aligning those desirable outcomes down into the processes, tasks and inputs of your organization.

Indeed, we have tackled a large part of "ethics by design" by starting with what value your organization adds to society, and stepping through a process for clearly articulating that and planning for desired impact. Let's now extend this model to ethics *within* your organization.

Endnotes

1. 2006—podcast by McDonough

2. Kaufman details these in 2000, 2006a,b. A specific, short treatment on what these three levels are and how they align can be found in Moore, Ellsworth, and Kaufman, 2008.

3. This comes from an NPR interview with Peter Orszag - "Budget Chief: For health care, more is not better"—April 16, 2009. http://www.npr.org/templates/story/story.php?storyId=103153156. Accessed April 16, 2009. While it is not clear whether the Obama administration will maintain an actual focus on measurable Outcomes, as suggested by Orszag's statements, the emphasis on "results" other than standard organizational-level results is notable. I would go further to suggest that the administration would be well-served to adopt a clear framework for effective planning that would allow them to distinguish more clearly between ends (Outcomes) and means (processes)—this is the logic underlying the statement that doing more isn't always doing better, also stated as the difference between doing the right things and doing things right. Additionally, the Mega model would clearly lay out for them the levels, or layers, of objectives and different types of results that a system or organization delivers.

4. Ibid

5. Ibid

6. A vibrant leader might even go further to say he or she wants to raise the general health of the public, not just maintain the status quo, and will track the positive impact on health by following rates on weight loss, cardio-vascular disease, and other indicators among their consumer base.

7. For more on writing effective objectives, consult any of the following resources. For Mega, Macro, Micro alignment, see Moore, Ellsworth & Kaufman, (2008). See also chapter 2 of *Mega Planning* (2000) by Kaufman, or *Performance by Design* (2005) by Watkins, *Preparing Instructional Objectives* (1997) by Mager, and *Analyzing Performance Problems* (1997) by Mager & Pipe.

Chapter 4
Defining Excellence: Ethics in Performance Standards

"...world-class ethics to accompany their world-class knowledge..."

Research findings on what businesses look
for in employees, Procario-Foley and Bean[1]

I know many readers would be disappointed to pick up a book with a title like this one and not find any information on ethics *within* the organization, so here we go. Organizations are looking at the results of employees who make unethical decisions, and companies are increasingly expressing a focus on "ethics" as a characteristic or performance standard of the people they hire. And yet, defining excellence standards *in ethics* for employees is as slick as mud. Indeed, ethical behavior within an organization is distinct from the ethical impacts of an organization, but the ethical behavior within is also largely a derivative of the ethical leadership and planning. So we have to start with organizational accountability—what are the socially responsible outcomes for which your organization is held accountable. This accountability, however, extends down to those within your organization and becomes a defining performance standard for what constitutes excellence within as well as without.

We have gone from the outside of the organization to inside the organization ("outside-in" planning).

If social responsibility is truly strategically planned for and then aligned down into an organization, we arrive at the point where we address alignment down into processes and employee activities. And in many ways, defining desired performance for employees is the same process, on a smaller scale, as defining desired organizational performance. When you start with clearly stated expectations and performance standards, you can chart a course to the desired end state.

In the many examples cited in this book, and those not cited but investigated for this book, the breakdown that led to a Mega-level, or societal, failure can often be traced from the leadership down into the bowels of an organization to procedures or decision points.

After initial bowing or crumbling of a bridge structure was noted, there was no follow up or corrective procedures, and there was a fatal failure of a major interstate artery. A procedure which could have prevented negative societal-level impact broke down.

When contaminated drinking water led to hundreds being infected with salmonella in Colorado,[2] somewhere down the line in the organization a safety check or procedure failed or someone failed to follow it properly.

Mega-level, or societal level, objectives for desirable impacts on society are only so good as how deeply they are planned down into the bowels of your organization. One way to think about the alignment between Mega, Macro and Micro objectives is how individual performance adds up to organizational performance, which adds up to external performance.

Mega-Macro-Micro Performance Alignment[3]

Mega-level considerations	What results does our organization contribute to the long-term success, survival, self-sufficiency, and quality of life of partners, stakeholders, clients, and clients' clients?
Macro-level considerations	What results do we contribute to the long-term success of our organization?
Micro-level consideration	What results do I contribute to the team or unit in which I work?

Your organization will have a negative impact on disease or illness if there are no checks during the production process for whether mercury is used in production of equipment or whether lead is used in product manufacturing. Your organization won't decrease deaths due to equipment failures if you don't have a good quality check procedure in place that all employees agree is important and understand why they do it (i.e., how that procedure adds value up the chain).

Ethics have increasingly been regarded as one of the key aspects to defining *exemplary* performance. In recent decades, the desirability for employees to exhibit ethical behavior has grown significantly, from almost no company listing ethics as a desired trait in the 1960s to over 60% stating ethics as among the top characteristics they look for.[4] Costly public failures determined to be breakdowns in ethics have been the primary driver for this change.[5] Much of the literature on ethics tends to focus on behaviors such as taking bribes, copyright infringement, accessibility issues, whistle blowing and so forth. This book has not focused on those sorts of topics (nor will it now), although that does not mean they are unimportant topics. However, these "issues" can become an end unto themselves, as organizations get lost in processes and focus on doing things right, but not doing the right things. The primary focus is on how individual decisions and behaviors add or detract value up the line.

Often, when organizations say they are interested in looking at "ethics" they mean they want to change the behaviors or performance of *individuals* within the organization. Let's get one thing very clear at the beginning of this chapter—individual performance and behavior is very complex, and research shows that 80-90% of individual performance in organizations stems from systemic characteristics (i.e. how your organization is designed) and not from individual characteristics such as knowledge or skills. So, while the individual certainly is a portion of variability in the equation, they only account for 10-20% of the variability.[6] The rest comes down to organizational design. This is like looking at ethics through an "ecosystems" lens.

While we'll look a bit at training (the intervention that addresses individual performance), I would not be doing you any service at all to pretend that some sort of training on ethics will significantly impact the performance within and of your organization. It may be a part of a set of interventions, but the truism certainly fits that training is necessary but not sufficient. In this chapter, we will explore a systemic model for performance interventions that includes, but is not limited to, training.

So, before you dismiss the emphasis of this book on systemic ethics too quickly and slip into the ease of focusing on individuals, keep in mind that even when we look internally, ethics in performance terms are more a result of how your organization is designed. Is there something about your organization that fosters or protects unethical behavior, or is there something about your organization that promotes ethical decision making? We'll take a look at those systemic features, or parts within an organization, that promote increased or decreased ethical performance of individuals since the systemic features of your organization account for a vast amount of the variability of the performance of your individual employees.

Going Internal

There are two ways to look at ethics *within* an organization. We will address both in this chapter.

Your Impact on Employees

The first way is to look at the impact of an organization on its employees. Your organization delivers results not only to external clients and society, but also to the members of society whom you hire as employees. How does your organization impact your employees' quality of life? Do you provide a healthy environment that does not damage their physical health? Do you, for example, locate employees in a building with mold or ventilation problems that can lead to health problems? Any organization of any type can face lawsuits from employees when the organization doesn't tend to the well-being of employees. However, when an organization delivers desirable results to its employees, people stay—turnover decreases or disappears entirely, loyalty and productivity increase, and an organization enjoys many benefits such as little time lost to sick leave or new market niches because of employees who are motivated to be and stay innovative. The measures of social responsibility presented in this book represent some of the same factors in human resources/industrial design literature showing a correlation to increased retention, on-the-job satisfaction, and productivity among employees.

As an organization, you plan for and deliver these results much the same as the previous strategic planning addressed. It's not enough to assume or hope for desired results. If you care, get the facts—and make the necessary changes when your data tells you there are necessary changes to be made. Your organization can plan for safe, healthy work environments—is the government building you're in safe? Can people get out quickly in case of emergency? Is that library basement space really inhabitable space for human beings, or should offices be located elsewhere? And the cost to your organization in these matters isn't measured just in terms of lawsuits for unsafe environments, but also is measured in terms of turnover or attrition. Have you lost a third of your faculty in the past three years? If so, you are actually driving away employees who care about quality—enough to make significant life changes to pursue quality environments. Those are the people you want to *keep,* because they are the people who can identify quality and be a part of defining exemplary performance. Instead, your organization may be inadvertently retaining the employees who care least about impact and quality, and that shows up in what your organization produces and delivers.

So the same set of external deliverables we looked at in Chapters 2 and 3 are the very same sort of deliverables you plan for with your employees. The better you plan for and consistently improve your organizational performance in this area, the more you will attract and retain the desired workforce.

Performance of Employees within Your Organization

The second way is to look at the ethical decisions of employees within organizations—this is the way ethics are most commonly addressed (although this book should have proven to you by now this is only a small fraction of the problem). Embezzlement, copyright infringement, and other similar employee behaviors are the most common targets of ethics "efforts" in organizations. Because, what organizations really are wanting to address when they talk about ethics is *behavior* (or more correctly, performance), and not *beliefs*, we continue with a performance-based treatment of ethics and look at employee behavior that is labeled as "ethical" or "unethical," much the same way other employee behaviors or performance can be examined.

By now we have essentially developed a full model of ethics by design—when organizations integrate ethics as a performance standard, both external and internal. Let's explore that model now. It helps us situate internal ethics and employee performance standards as a part of story.

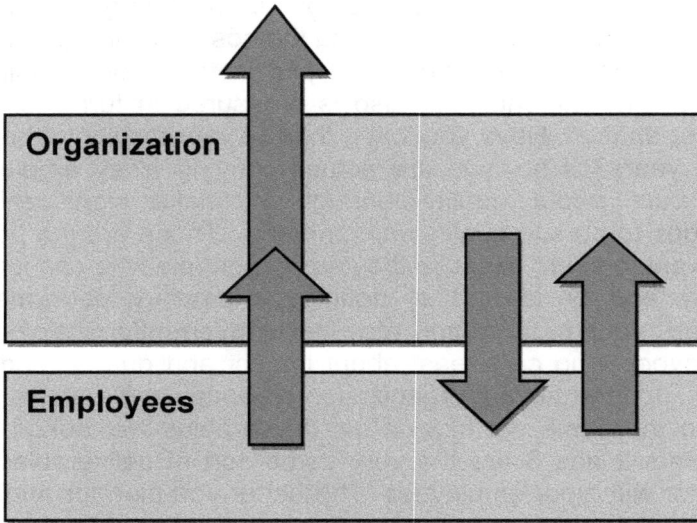

Ethics by Design: A Planning and Performance-Based Model of Ethics

The model put forth in this book is one of value-added—the value your organization delivers to external clients and society, and the value your employees add up the organizational chain (Mega, Macro, and Micro alignment). We also look at the value-added of your organization internally to your employees, and of the value employees add to your organization.

Truly strategic planning addresses desired results. That is represented by the vertically aligned arrows in the visual depiction: the value your organization adds starts from inside your organization and then is delivered to external clients and society. These are the 13 measures of societal impact we've covered. The arrow going down from the organization to employees represents the same deliverables from your organization to individuals. The 13 measures of societal impact are results your organization also delivers to your employees for which you can plan. The arrow going up from employees to the organization represents employee performance that either adds or detracts value from the organization internally. Employees who steal money, actively discriminate through their positions of authority, or ignore guidelines and thereby contribute to unsafe working environments detract value from the organization. Conversely, employees who make sure procedures that ensure safety are followed or developed and implemented, or employees who actively decrease discrimination during hiring and firing practices, add value to your organization.

Delivering Desirable Results to Employees

Because this is essentially the same content the whole book has been addressing, this section will be relatively condensed. The impact of your organization on employees can be measured by the same indicators from Kaufman's Mega model. An organization has a positive or negative impact on the health, well-being, and quality of life for its employees. The question isn't whether your organization impacts employees, but whether it has planned for desired impact on the individuals who are a part of your organization.

Obvious impacts include health and well-being, such as the safety of employees. This includes not only safety in terms of proper disposal of toxic materials, but also the overall condition of work environments. Restaurants and food packaging operations handle these sorts of issues every day. However, organizations like hospitals and schools are also beginning to redesign buildings so the structures are physically beneficial rather than physically detrimental. If employees are getting sick because of mold in the walls, toxic fumes in a building, asbestos, etc., this leads to increased sickness and time missed for work due to illness, which leads to a decrease in productivity and an increase in insurance rates.

Not-so-obvious impacts include forms of discrimination that lead to decreased self-sufficiency or quality of life for employees. One growing example is the notion of flexibility in response to diversity of life arrangements among employees.[7] More employees are taking care of both aging parents and children still at home. Many more single parents increasingly enter the workforce as well. Along with their skills, these employees bring different life arrangements that demand different solutions from the 8:00–5:00 work schedule. Organizations that adapt and offer flexible scheduling, telecommuting, and job sharing are able to tap a broader pool of applicants and attract a highly-committed workforce that appreciates the organization's responsiveness. Without this flexibility, employees with life arrangements that don't fit the 8:00–5:00 schedule have fewer opportunities—due to external or irrelevant characteristics rather than actual job competency, and thus face a form of discrimination and as a result have a lower quality of life and in many cases cannot achieve self-sufficiency.

However, when an organization plans specifically for employee diversity, and as a result develops flexible policies and infrastructures to support a variety of work schedules, it then has a purposeful positive impact on the quality of life for employees.[8]

Organizational planning for these sorts of desired results, as stated, is akin to the strategic planning process. A measurable ethics objective in your organization becomes the health of your employees, and self-sufficiency and quality of life for diverse employees. These objectives can be stated in terms like:

"No employee of our organization shall fall ill due to toxic work environments or suffer from injury or death due to unsafe work environments, as indicated by reports of illness, injury or death to the human resources and corroborated by independently-verifiable physicians' reports."

"No employee within our organization will earn less than his or her peer due to race, gender, sexual orientation, creed, disability, life circumstances, or other irrelevant characteristics that are not related to job performance, as indicated by analyses of payrolls, promotions and advancement statistics, and hiring and firing statistics."

"No student within our school will become sick or die as a result of the food served in the cafeteria, nor shall any student in our school be located in an unhealthy or unsafe environment, such as any unsafe laboratories, classrooms, or housing facilities as indicated by injuries, death or illnesses that can be traced to toxic material or adverse conditions as determined by an outside auditing agency."

Like the Mega-level objectives for what your organization delivers to society, these objectives articulate measurable value-added to the employees of your organization. Your employees are, after all, members of society. What you deliver to them is exactly what you deliver to society. Organizations that add this sort of measurable value to employees enjoy a more committed, productive workforce that gives back to the organization.

Employee Performance: Setting Standards and Designing the Performance Environment

As noted earlier, most of the discussion around ethics in organizations refers to behaviors and acts of individual employees— or to the *performance* of employees. In an attempt to address individual performance, many organizations develop codes of ethics or workshops on ethics. Others conclude this can't be effectively addressed because of the individual nature of morals and values.

If we define ethics in performance terms, then we can design for desired performance.

In order to address ethical performance in your organizations, we have to first start by shifting our understanding of ethics from one that centers on personal beliefs and values or moral reasoning to a practical understanding that centers on consequences or results. Organizations aren't, and can't rightly be, in the business of selecting employees based on personal beliefs or values. They can, however, be in the business of retaining employees who yield desirable results—which includes the ability to complete a necessary job function as well as the ability to bring about desirable consequences. Results are entirely independent from an individual's beliefs. This represents a move from belief-based perspective to a perform-ance-based perspective of ethics.

In order to achieve exemplary performance, you first have to establish clear performance expectations.[9] We tend to be really good at defining specific tasks we want people to do. Watkins notes this is the act of defining *performing* as opposed to *performance*. When we define *performance*, we actually begin to define the results of people's tasks and activities and use of resources. We can define *performing* all day long and do a great job of getting people to do things, but it is only when we shift our focus to *performance* and to the results of those activi-ties that we can actually provide guidance to employees and leaders on how they should perform, and engage in continual improvement over time.

So the first step is identifying very clear performance expec-tations that relate to desired results. This is a radically different approach from developing a code of ethics. Codes of ethics tend to sound something like "our organization values diversity and makes every effort to support diversity"—warm, fuzzy, and meaningless. Defined in terms of performance, however, an organization can state:

> "No employee shall engage in any activities that put fellow employees or external clients in danger of injury or illness, including ignoring operational procedures specifically designed to fully test all programming language for failures (or all engine prototypes, and so on) prior to implementation."

> "All employees will follow proper disposal or removal procedures of hazardous waste and personal clean up as indicated by zero incidents of contamination, illness or death due to the hazardous materials in this envi-ronment (although an organization could also choose to plan that there are no hazardous materials present in any of the work employees do)."

"No employee shall engage in hiring, firing or management practices that purposefully or inadvertently lead to the promotion or retention of individuals based on irrelevant factors such as age, race, gender, sexual orientation, family arrangement, or religion, as indicated by consistent analysis of data on hiring, promotion and salary equity, both internally and in relation to national data and trends."

Now *that* is a code of ethics that actually means something and can drive performance.

Let's examine this in the context of a case study.

A Bug in the Code: How a Procedural Breakdown Leads to a Systemic Failure with Negative Consequences

Dave had decided to stay at the office overnight to hang around on suicide watch, not a normal shift description for their central office. However, a few of the programmers in the shop working on some updates to the code had skipped a final test phase of the prescribed process and implemented some code in the state-wide healthcare network that turned out to have an error. In some last-second polishing to tested code, a programmer had dropped a semi-colon in the code that caused the whole script to crash. But since they had tested every other step along the way, and these additions were "small," they ran with the script. As a result of the update, some equipment for critically ill patients stopped working. When news reached the programmers, they were distraught—they were now working furiously to correct the problem, but they were clearly distressed as well. Dave was immediately dialed at home and rushed to the office to get on the problem. Once there, he found two programmers typing like mad, eyes wide open, barely blinking, in complete silence except for the sound of the keys clicking on the keyboard. One in particular was somber, pale, and looked to Dave like he could snap at any second. Since there were only a few programmers who knew the code and could fix the problem, Dave had to keep these guys on the floor until the problem was

(continued)

A Bug in the Code (continued)

solved. But he also decided he had to be sure he kept close tabs on his crew for the night and a few days to come.

The seriousness of the situation was unavoidable, but Dave also decided that yet another death should not result from this incident—either patients or staff. While the staff had to take responsibility for the consequences, Dave decided that part of taking responsibility was fixing the problem before anything further happened. And perhaps the only way through their despair was to be a core part of the solution. He was direct that this was a major failure, but quick to emphasize that things would be even worse if the programmers didn't focus and work to get things fixed ASAP. "You know what you did wrong," Dave said, "but get over it because you don't have time for a pity party—there are still people depending on your success. So go succeed." Dave stayed there, ordered some food and drinks for them, and worked with them to problem-solve, and even just joke and talk a bit. Four hours later, the problem was resolved and no further deaths had resulted. At 5 a.m., Dave sent the men home—he wanted them to rest but told them he would call during the day to check on them, too.

The mood in the central office among the programming staff changed dramatically after that. Many of them had been fairly new out of college or local technical schools. It was a relatively young team who had viewed programming as their "art form." But after this incident, suddenly the reason for procedures and certain steps in the procedures were very clear. The team seemed to be much more sober about their work. Additionally, their language shifted. They talked about patients more, referred to them as people in very human terms, and referred to their work as serving these people. The direct relationship between their work and the humans in beds in hospitals around the state was now very clear, as was the impact of their work on those people. From then on, the consequences of decisions to real people "out there" were a part of every decision-making process going forward. When updates were about to be rolled out, the staff mapped out clear procedures for testing code so that "nobody dies this time." They even asked Dave to create a simulated environment and identify partners in hospitals around

(continued)

A Bug in the Code (concluded)

the state to work with in testing implementations before going state-wide. They set a target that nobody should die ever again as a result of their products and procedures, and even raised the bar to say that no equipment should fail as a result, regardless of whether that resulted in a death or not.

Over time, Dave also noticed that staff turnover rates dropped to low levels. In the initial aftermath, some staff had left, deciding they just didn't want to work in a high-stakes environment. But those that stayed really stayed—and new staff was inducted into this culture of consequences. A fairly recent hire stopped by Dave's office one day and commented, "This is a unique place from other places I've worked. People here actually care." Dave reflected on this—indeed, they did care, and not just in words but in action.

Often, individuals will see the disconnect between what they do every day and the impact on the outside world. And yet, we experience the failures of those disconnects in instances like this. When employees overlook critical procedures like quality check processes, they run the risk of overlooking a bug in the code, a crack in the concrete, or a deadly bacteria in the food. Dave's experience highlights how we can make ethics practical and how they are a part of optimal performance.

Consider how Dave handled these disastrous events. How were procedures and processes aligned upward to Mega-level objectives? What role did Dave play in creating a culture of consequences? How do Dave's decisions reflect a consequences framework? How could your staff integrate a consequences framework into decision making? What characteristics reflect a staff that is committed to applied ethics? What characteristics reflect a manager who is committed to applied ethics? What characteristics reflect an organization that is committed to applied ethics?

Ethics by Design: Organizational Performance Model to Support Ethical Performance by Employees

Once you have clearly defined objectives for ethical performance within your organization, then it's time to look at how you design the different layers of your organization to support that desired performance.

Most organizations jump to training or workshops on ethics as a means for "increasing ethics" in their organization, as indicated by the plethora of case studies or anecdotes in literature detailing training programs on ethics. But workshops and training address only one performance barrier: knowledge/skills. And lack of knowledge/skills only account for 10–20% of the variance of how individuals perform in your organization.[10] There are two ways to impact this portion of the equation in your employees: selection (who are you hiring to begin with) and training (aiding the employees you have in continuing to develop desired knowledge and skills).

Five other interventions account for the remaining 80–90% of variance in employee performance.[11] So let's start with an overview of training on ethics and move through that to a robust, performance-based model of ethics within an organization. Training may be a necessary part of your plan, but by no means is it sufficient (and if you plan to address any performance issues through training alone, you are almost guaranteed to fail unless a quality needs analysis reveals that, in fact, the *only* gap is a gap in knowledge/skills).

What We Know about Ethics Training So Far

As a result of growing ethical issues and research findings on performance and ethics, companies began identifying ethics as one of the most desirable traits they look for when hiring new employees. That demand, in turn, affected business programs in higher education, as they had to adapt by developing courses in business ethics. In a 1992 survey of businesses, 63% reported that a "sense of social, professional and ethical responsibility" was one of the most sought-after qualities in graduates of business programs.[12] Ten years later, businesses were still reporting that they wanted employees to possess "world-class ethics to accompany their world-class knowledge."[13] It is not enough to have employees who have certain skills, but employees must be able to make sound decisions that lead to desirable results. This is only increasingly true as the networks of society become more global and interwoven. In addition, thanks to Sarbanes-Oxley and Federal Sentencing Guidelines, ethics have become a part of training departments and higher education curricula around the country. But do people really change their behavior based on a workshop they attend during their workday, or because of a class that meets degree requirements?

From an instructional standpoint, the question of whether a person even (a) retains the information over time and (b) knows how to apply the knowledge highlights a broad variability of likely success dependent upon how the instructional environment is designed. On-the-job transfer is an area of much research and discussion, as training has consistently failed to deliver the desired results. Research on retention (i.e., did it stick in their heads) and transfer (i.e. can they use their knowledge) shows that some instructional approaches work better than others. Among the worst in terms of long-term retention and transfer is the instructional approach of lecture (regardless of whether it's direct lecture or lecture by PowerPoint). However, this is the most prevalent approach. Learners receive a great deal of information, and maybe only 10% of it sticks. Use of multimedia can improve that—but only if the media is designed according to sound, research-based principles. Most multi-media used in learning environments, including text books, does not meet this definition. So even if training is selected as an intervention, to have any sort of efficacy it must be based on research-based principles that account for how people learn and how transfer of knowledge occurs.

Some research in business ethics demonstrates that practitioners who have been trained in ethics do perform better on the job and tend to have higher rates of productivity.[14] However, the *degree* of impact of training or education in ethics is another matter altogether. Even if an individual has some foundational knowledge or requisite skills, those characteristics are not enough to overcome the environment or climate of a given organization. As Dale Brethower states, "If you pit a good employee against a bad system, the system will win every time."[15] This is strongly evidenced by the statistics at the beginning of the book on how many employees have seen but not reported unethical behavior.

Dobne, Ritchie, and Zerbe examined the relationship between organizational value systems and employee productivity. Employees in organizations that possessed values related to social responsibility tended to express statistically significant higher commitment to the organization and positive affect about their work (two constructs that measure productivity) than employees in organizations with other value systems.[16] What this suggests is that organizational climate and leadership greatly impact employee behavior. Organizations with clear, strong social responsibility also attract like-minded employees. Additionally, these findings indicate that organizational leadership, not any particular training program, influence the ethical climate of an organization.

Research in business ethics also showed that the way ethics were implemented or modeled made a difference in the ethical behavior of employees. It is not enough to have a code of ethics, and it is not enough to punish employees when they fail to adhere to the code.[17] Weaver has delineated two forms of ethics training in organizations: compliance-orientation and value-orientation.[18] In compliance-orientation training, leadership establishes the ethics then enforces rules and monitors behaviors. Employees can be punished for not adhering to ethical codes. Compliance-orientation training has less impact on employee behavior, because employees become cynical about the rules if leaders don't model the ethical standards themselves.

In value-orientation training, ethics are defined by the entire organization, with commitment from management and support and trust for employees. In such training, the emphasis is on helping employees develop decision-making skills so they avoid unethical behavior that could tarnish a company's reputation.[19]

Value-orientation ethics programs contributed more to desired behavior in employees.[20] These findings suggest that leadership in and modeling of ethical behavior, versus simply demanding it, has a greater impact on the ethical behavior of employees. Translating into educational institutions, these findings suggest that students will exhibit more ethical behavior if faculty or teachers model that same behavior (for a more extensive, excellent exposition based in education environments, see Matchett[21]).

Leadership isn't carried out through training programs, but instead is carried out through the system—through the characteristics of your organization. Leadership translates into policies, consequences, rewards/incentive systems, the resources that are (or are not) leveraged, and so forth. Whether you are CEO (or CIO or CFO), a mid-level manager, a project manager, a unit coordinator, or simply manager of your own workstation, the policies, rewards, etc., that you implement communicate your leadership and create a specific sort of climate for ethical performance (or lack of ethical performance).

Let's look at the systemic characteristics and how you can leverage those to design an environment that enhances or supports ethical performance.

A System Approach to an Individual Problem

In the preface to the book, I commented that this book is not just about changing individuals. For nearly as long as ethics has been a topic of interest, the focus has primarily (though not entirely) been on the individual—how does the individual make a decision, how do individuals grow in their moral reasoning, why does one person make one choice and another person another choice, how do we get individuals in an organization to behave more ethically. I contend not that these inquiries have been misguided or have been a waste of time, but rather that the paradigm of systemic thinking has ushered in a new way of thinking about the domain of ethics, one that requires individuals to align what they use, do, produce, and deliver with external clients and society. A culture of ethics is vital for such alignment.

Systemic thinking has already yielded great insights into how human organizations function. The International Society for Performance Improvement specifically encourages its membership to adopt a systemic approach to solving human performance problems.[22] As I've continually noted, research has shown that only 10-20% of performance gaps are due to individual performance. The vast majority of undesirable performance results from system features.[23]

Trevino has proposed an empirically-based approach for "developing and/or changing the organization's ethics culture to support and encourage ethical behavior in an organization."[24] For Trevino, the ethics culture is a result of interaction between formal and informal systems, and those systems support either ethical or unethical behavior. Her work has identified six formal and five informal characteristics of organizational systems. The formal characteristics include leadership, structure, policies, reward systems, orientation and training programs, and decision-making processes. These areas overlap with the performance-based model of ethics this book proposes below. The informal characteristics include norms, heroes and models, rituals, myths, sagas and stories, and language. According to Trevino, the formal characteristics create and maintain the culture, while the informal characteristics keep that culture alive and provide a point for validating or invalidating the formal characteristics. For example, a story or myth floating around the work environment that contradicts a reward system or decision-making process would lead employees to question the formal system's validity.

As Watkins explains in his book, *Performance by Design*, we can design for desired performance when we take a systemic approach and clearly differentiate between "performing" and "performance." It is the difference between action and results—between tasks or procedures that your employees follow and what results from those tasks or procedures. Performing is the doing; performance is the results. Quality testing code before it's released is a procedure—that is performing. Having no down time or failed equipment as a result of bad code is a result—that's performance.

Watkins presents a full account of how to clearly define and design towards desired performance.[25] Given his treatment, what I present here is a shorter explanation of the process meant more to address the question of whether ethics can be treated in performance/behavioral terms.

A sound process for designing for desired performance starts like we did in Chapter 2—by clearly defining the gap. To address employee performance, you must first start by clearly articulating how you want them to perform. Once that is defined, a needs assessment will determine your employees' current or actual performance. When those two data points are established, then you have identified a gap—the distance between desired and actual performance.

To move actual performance towards desired performance, there are a suite of interventions from which you can choose. Often, you will likely be using a number of interventions in conjunction with each other. Behavior is a complex matter, so the organizational design that supports desired behavior is usually more complex than just a two-hour training video. The range of interventions is represented below, situated in the context of strategic planning.[26]

VISION (Mega-level Objective)

Mission (Macro)	Mission (Macro)	Mission (Macro)

Micro	Micro	Micro	Micro	Micro	Micro	Micro	Micro	Micro

Performance Interventions:
Barriers to or Supports for
Organizational Processes

Rewards & Incentives

Job/Task Expectations & Clarifications

Resources/ Support Tools

Policy

Skills & Knowledge

Consequences & Feedback

Products

Desired Impact & Results

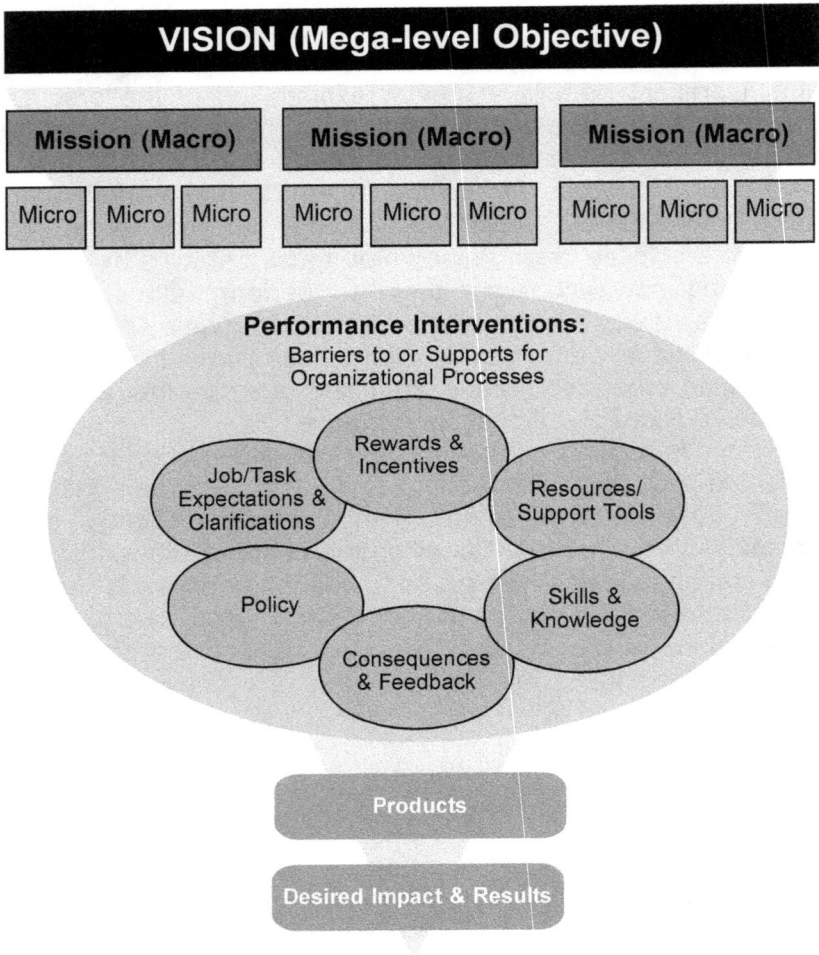

We have spent a great deal of time on Vision, Mission and Objectives in this book. Once you have clearly defined objectives—for your organization and for employee performance (like all the examples provided in this book)—then you can conduct a gap analysis to determine what the current, or actual, performance of your employees are. Once the gap has been identified, the next step is to analyze contributing factors—figure out *why* the gap exists. Without this step, you can waste a great deal of time and money. This is why there are so many training programs—and why many of them don't work. Once a gap is identified, most folks assume it's because employees lack the requisite knowledge or skills to perform the tasks correctly. This is probably not the case. For example, a manager sets a goal for his sales team to increase their sales by 20% in the third quarter. By the end of the third quarter, sales are actually down by 2%. The manager then decides that his employees should get some training. Even after the training, though, sales are still down. An end-of-workshop learning assessment reveals that the sales team understands the concepts, yet they're not increasing their sales. Wanting to find out why the sales folks aren't working harder on sales, the manager decides to open an anonymous feedback box. Employees explained that to increase the number of sales, they had to work longer hours, but that didn't translate into additional income for them. In short, there was a lack of incentive—not a lack of skills or knowledge. No amount of training was going to change that.

Ethics defined in performance terms are much the same. Employees will perform a certain way because of policies that encourage or discourage certain behaviors, because there are no incentives or because there are actually disincentives, or even because they don't have adequate resources, tools, or feedback channels. The encapsulated set of Performance Interventions in the model address how you plan for desired ethical performance (indeed, any type of performance) of your employees in your organization.

Just as the Vision must be aligned with the Mission and organizational objectives (Mega, Macro, Micro), so that alignment continues on down into the selection of performance interventions. The "performance support system" represented by the six modules should be configured as a direct result of what you want to get out of the employees and the organization as a whole as defined in your vision, mission and objectives.

Let's look at each Performance Intervention and how it applies in designing for desirable *ethical* performance in employees:

**Resources/
Support Tools**

Resources or lack thereof can be a significant barrier to performance. Consider whether there are adequate infrastructure, personnel, monetary, and other sorts of resources. If not, this could be a reason for undesirable performance in employees. This is separate from skills or knowledge—employees may know full well how to do something or that something is wrong, but if they lack resources, that can become a problem.

Resources can take the form of tools or processes, as well as the lack of funding to get the right tools and processes in place. Lack of tools, a bad environment, or fuzzy processes can lead to poor performance. If a graphic designer doesn't have the right software to get his or her job done, she or he isn't going to perform well no matter how well he or she understands the expectations or how much knowledge and skills he or she has. Consider whether a certain tool in the environment or a better process could promote ethical behavior. One of the more commonly cited reasons that people do not report unethical behavior is because they're unclear just what to do or to whom to report it. Additionally, processes or procedures that employees follow may lack definition or steps that relate to ethical performance. Is there an adequate testing procedure or quality check process before a product or code leaves the central office or the factory floor? Is there a system for students to report abusive faculty behavior without fear of retribution. . .and leading to the next intervention, do students or employees see that these processes actually work?

Job/Task Expectations & Clarifications

The "not my job" or "not in my job description" mindset is a major barrier to desired performance. When it comes to ethics, employees may be saying that a certain procedure isn't their job, or they're not paid enough to intervene in a situation involving, for example, sexual harassment or discrimination.

How an individual's job and tasks are defined can greatly impact just how they perform. Expectations have to be clear and communicated not just in a job description but in ongoing performance evaluations, as well.

In a nutshell, this is about how employees receive information about what's expected of them and how they're doing as they go. **Feedback** systems tend to be under-developed, and yet feedback is essential to performance. When an employee under-performs, or performs exceptionally, does he or she know it? A faculty member once explained that the only way he knew if he was doing a good job or not was whether his contract was renewed every four years. That's a large gap of time during which many things can happen, or not happen. How often do employees receive feedback about performance? Do they know what's expected of them?

Rewards & Incentives

People will not change their behavior if there is no reason to. In fact, we often continue destructive behaviors because there is incentive to, despite other possible disincentives. **Rewards, recognition and incentives** address a part of why individuals are willing to change their behaviors. If individuals are continually chastised or ridiculed in meetings for trying to ensure that the products or services you deliver don't have a negative impact, then there's a problem with rewards, recognition and incentives. If your employees wind up having to out themselves as a "rat" to report unethical behavior, then chances are high that serious indiscretions are going unreported in your organization. Consider whether employees in your organization are rewarded for ethical, or unethical, behavior. If your most unethical employees are making more money or getting highlighted in meetings or newsletters, then you are promoting unethical behavior— regardless of how inadvertent that may be.

Consequences & Feedback

Consequences are just that—what happens as a result of what you do. These can seem tightly related to rewards and incentives, but in fact are quite distinct. Let's use an example for educational systems just to drive home the point these are relevant, regardless of what type of organization you work in.

Let's say your school does not ensure it provides access to the curriculum for learners with disabilities. The consequences start local and short-term and grow into global and long-term consequences. That child does not learn what he or she could, and therefore doesn't progress, and isn't able to go on and get a job after graduation. The school demonstrates a less-than-100% achievement level, which could impact funding or performance on state or national tests. The parents are then left supporting more than might have otherwise been necessary, maxing out their support structure. They have to request funds for support, which means they draw funds from some sort of government program. At this point, this is more expensive than what was necessary to invest during the educational process. The general society is now having to invest even more to support individuals who could have been self-sufficient had the educational subsystem adopted the policies and approaches that said we will give every individual possible access to learning and, therefore, access to a self-sufficient life. The cost for government programs that support these individuals is far more expensive after the fact.

Let's say the flip side is true. The consequences for a student with disabilities succeeding in your school means your school shows better results on state or national assessments and, therefore, maintains or gets an increase in funding. Additionally, the individual student is learning, feeling more and more empowered in what they can do, and goes on to achieve more. The parents feel their burden lighten, even if only slightly. The student goes on to graduate and, even though he has an IQ of 60, is happily and gainfully employed for what looks to be the rest of his adulthood, and even moves out into an apartment of his own, has his own social life going to ball games with friends, and is contributing to society rather than having to depend on social programs. The individual is self-sufficient and feeling empowered to be so, and the rest of the support system around him isn't tapped.

(Before you dismiss "the flip side," that description is based on an actual individual who benefitted from a system that focused on supporting him for optimal performance.)

Skills & Knowledge

Skills & Knowledge is the *only* one out of the six that can be defined on an individual basis. An individual either has the skills and/or knowledge or does not. All the rest are system characteristics that result from decisions. If undesired performance is due to a lack in skills or knowledge, the solution is training. However, if it's not due to a lack in skills or knowledge, all the training in the world won't solve the problem, because the solution doesn't fit the problem.

On the front end, lack of skills and knowledge is addressed through selection. Like the saying in real estate (that it's all about "location, location, location"), employee performance all starts with "selection, selection, selection." However, we all know that environments change, and we ask our existing staff to remain nimble and responsive to changes. Thus, training does emerge as one possible solution to support ongoing performance.

So there is a time and a place for training—it's just not all the time, for every performance problem. An effective gap analysis will assist you in determining whether this is an appropriate fit.

Additionally, most of the literature on ethics training focuses solely on training employees about ethics. In truth, the necessary training may not be necessarily about "ethics," per se, as we are used to traditionally thinking about it. As you gather data on actual performance, it could be that a procedure has to be adapted or changed to ensure more errors are caught on the assembly line, or a change in equipment will reduce errors that lead to failures of your product out in the world. In those instances, employees will be receiving training on new procedures or equipment that leads to desired societal impact and results. We do not necessarily have to turn employees into students of ethics to promote ethical performance.

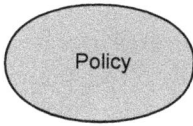

Policy

I end with **Policy** because this is a significant domain that dramatically impacts performance. However, it can be one of the hardest ones to get right. Clearly, there are books upon books on policy, so this is a light treatment. And yet, in short, it could be argued this book is all about policy. Your vision statement is your policy. As one state's Secretary of Education once stated, "personnel is policy." We establish and carry out policy in a number ways, besides just the policy documents a committee writes.

Policies can pose a significant barrier to performance, especially when they detail consequences or disincentives that drive people away from desired performance. Many universities face challenges encouraging faculty to adopt innovative tools or practices, for example, because policies on promotion and tenure wind up punishing or deterring innovation.

A policy that requires all full-time employees to be in the office from 8:00–5:00, regardless of the job duties or the location of the employee, can be very problematic. I have seen policies much like that one actually limit an organization's ability to attract or retain the most talented workforce. For example, a set of employees were hired to manage different regions of the state. However, the employees were actually required to be in the central office Monday-Friday, 8:00–5:00. They literally could not perform their job functions.

Additionally, the policy did not allow any managers to offer employees flexible work schedules. This began to significantly impact employees who were single parents, who were caring for aging parents, or who had health issues that require they visit doctors during normal business hours. In other countries, policies based on "universal design" principles have been broadly adopted to facilitate more diversity within the workforce. Such universal design principles are an excellent example of how diversity can be treated practically: a policy is adopted that the employer (including governments and educational institutions) can and will provide flexible scheduling, telecommuting, and job sharing to accommodate a diverse workforce. Early literature indicates that universal design policies translate into higher productivity, higher employee commitment, and lower turnover rates.

Many companies are increasingly adopting universal design policies that apply both to the infrastructure and to the organizational structure (i.e., policy) of the organization. Organizations all the way from Fujitsu to the United Nations to Pacific Bell are establishing policies based on universal design that drive the development of their products, the sorts of activities they engage in, and how they set up work environments or establish foreign policy.

This is only one example, and there are many policies—all designed to impact performance one way or another. So as you consider the gaps between actual and desired perform-ance, you likely will wind up reviewing policies.

What may not be immediately obvious about these six sys-tem characteristics is just how scalable the concept is—both horizontally and vertically. These six characteristics apply within your department as well as to your organization or insti-tution as a whole. And these characteristics apply to a national ecosystem, not just to the organizations and institutions within the national framework. For example, the national policies of any given country will dramatically affect the ecosystem in which organizations and institutions can thrive and effectively pursue socially desirable ends. Just as organizations are systems unto themselves, they are also subsystems within the larger context of a political structure, and that political structure is yet another subsystem within the larger system of our global, shared society. In his book *Outliers*, Gladwell explains how exemplary performers grow from fertile ecosystems (2008). In the very same fashion, the success of organizations is not due solely to internal factors, but also stems from the drivers in the external system around it.[27] This growing awareness of the systemic, interrelated, and reciprocal relationship between various organizations (education, for-profit, and so forth) and the shape of society is inescapable in performance data, and is becoming inescapable as a planning model.

Potatoes, Peanuts, Spinach, Baby Bottles, Toys, and Beef: A Recipe for Organizational Failures. . .and Successes

In the span of less than a year, major national recalls were issued on all of the products listed—potatoes, peanuts, spin-ach, baby bottles, toys, beef—and many others on long lists of recalls.[28] On top of this sat the collapse of the mortgage and banking industries. It might create too much of a depressive picture to point out additional short-comings in other subsystems, such as criticisms of the educational and health-care systems in the US. These are all examples of the bi-directional relationship between planning at the top of an organization leading down to practices and processes within, that in turn yield specific products and results back up the organizational chain and on out to society.

The other way to frame the many "failures" we see is actually as a failure of a prevailing paradigm for planning and organizational leadership. Ethics by design is part of a set of alternative planning models that focus on creating change, rather than just managing it.

Additionally, the way to interpret these "failures" is that society simply demands exemplary performance by the organizations that are supposed to serve society, that function within it and want our business or votes or budget allocations. That is the essence of accountability, both external and internal. Externally, society and the larger marketplace expect organizations to deliver desirable results, not just desirable Products like loans or food or houses. The consequences of an organization delivering anything short of excellence are simply not good enough, so we are engaged in a constant process of continuous improvement at the societal level.

In fact, the very interconnected nature of all systems and organizations demands excellence from all. What is apparent is that planners and leaders actually do get that the failure of, say, AIG or other large entities will have ripple effects throughout many aspects of the system. What is tragic, though, is that we understand that interrelated nature in the context of failures rather than in the context of how to design for success. Organizations simply are not insular in their successes or failures: society cannot continue to thrive with anything short of excellence from the organizations within. When the cells within a body become too toxic, the body as a whole cannot overcome the effects. Society functions the same way, with all the organizations and entities operating within. In the face of toxic organizations, the environment cannot be sustained—people's health and well-being and ability to be self-sufficient cannot be sustained. Like any organic system that rejects or tries to fight off the negative effects, the societal-level system has a way of kicking out any part that doesn't work. The negative results and poor products get sent back to organizations or professions—a rejected design, a noted breach of contract. "Failures" are a way society says, "It's time for a new design."

Sam Ervin, a U.S. Senator best known for his investigating committees on Senator Joseph McCarthy and, later, on Watergate, stated, "A leader is someone who helps improve the lives of other people or improve the system they live under." That sort of leadership can occur from any level within a system—at the helm of an organization, in a department or unit within, or even in a local community. Historically, the organizations that stay in place for the long haul (decades, not just several quarters or years) are the ones who improve the lives of other people and improve the system. They create conditions for ideal change, or what Bernardez refers to as a "performance ecosystem,"[29] by starting with a vision of society and planning for how their organization fits in with that vision.

When we lose sight of our vision—our Ideal Vision—for society, we actually lose sight of where we are aiming our organizations. No wonder chaos ensues. This is the actual gauntlet that has been thrown down—by this book, by the dramatic failures of large systems in 2008 and 2009, by the numerous failures and shortcomings before then leading society to demand change: we can return to bad practices that have already evidenced where they lead, or we can stop doing business "the usual way" and transform our organizational practices.

The choice is up to us—we create the change (or we continue to be strategically tragic). By doing ethics on purpose—by design—we can create the change that we desire and enjoy organizational successes for the long-term.

Endnotes

1. Procario-Foley, E. & Bean, D. (2002). Institutions of higher educa-
    tion: Cornerstones in building ethical organizations. *Teaching
    Business Ethics, 6,* 101-116.

2. March 24, 2008—http://abcnews.go.com/Health/Germs/wire-
    Story?id=4511599; also reported in local outlets

3. Kaufman, 1992, 1998, 2000; Kaufman, et. al., 2001

4. This statistic comes from Hammond, 1992—an internal
    communication at Smeal College of Business, Pennsylvania
    State University, cited in . Dean (1993). A selected review of the
    underpinnings of ethics for human performance technology
    professionals—Part one: Key ethical theories and research.
    Performance Improvement Quarterly, 6(4), 6-32.

5. Davis, 1999—Davis explains what he calls the "ethics boom" in
    higher education curriculum. In short, professions like medicine,
    law, engineering and business were faced with ways to integrate
    practical ethics into curricula across the country after major public
    failures or increasingly complex decision-making confronted cur-
    rent and future professionals. While this "ethics boom" has led to
    the integration of ethics in curriculum, though, it is unclear
    whether that is translating into actual ethical performance.

6. Deming, Juran; also cite ISPI / HPT Handbook and emphasis on
    systemic design

7. Grzywacz, Casey, & Jones, 2007; Grzywacz, Carlson, Kacmar, &
    Wayne, 2007; Siegel, Mosca, & Karim, 1997

8. Ibid

9. (Watkins, 2007)—Performance by Design. In this portion of the
    book, I suggest that "ethics by design" is a performance-based
    approach to designing for desirable ethical performance. Thus, a
    well-grounded performance design model will enhance this sec-
    tion. Instead of going into greater detail, I touch on some of the

    linkages to the body of work by Watkins and other professional
    performance technologists. For more on professionals in the area
    of performance improvement, see also the International Society
    for Performance Improvement (www.ispi.org) which certifies per-
    formance technologists based on demonstrated evidence of
    adhering to standards that include systemic approaches to prob-
    lem solving.

10. Deming & Juran

11. The 80-90% figure is from Deming, Juran, cited previously. The six characteristics come from Watkins & Wedman, 2003, in press; Villachica & Stone, 1995 and the body of research in performance improvement that appears to be solidifying around these core systemic characteristics.

12. Hammond, J. (1992). Internal communication, Smeal College of Business, Pennsylvania State University, cited in P. Dean (1993). A selected review of the underpinnings of ethics for human performance technology professionals—Part one: Key ethical theories and research. *Performance Improvement Quarterly, 6*(4), 6-32.

13. Procario-Foley & Bean, 2002—Procario-Foley, E. & Bean, D. (2002). Institutions of higher education: Cornerstones in building ethical organizations. *Teaching Business Ethics, 6*, 101-116.

14. Delaney & Sockell, 1992—Delaney, J. & Sockell, D. (1992). Do company ethics training programs make a difference? An empirical analysis. *Journal of Business Ethics, 11*, 719-727.

15. Brethower, D, (2006). *Performance Analysis: Knowing What to Do and How.* Amherst, MA., HRD Press.

16. 2000—Dobni Ritchie and Zerbe

17. Dean, 1993—many have noted that "codes of ethics" tend to become window dressing in organizations—written documents that are filed away or maybe posted, but that don't serve any planning or performance function for the organization

18. Weaver, 1999

19. Harrington, 1991

20. Weaver, 1999

21. Matchett, 2008. Matchett is Director of the Institute for Professional Ethics at the University of Northern Colorado. In this article, she explores what she calls deliberate ethics. She asserts that ethics are taught and modeled, but we are often unconscious about how we approach them, or if we want to be deliberate are unsure about how to go about it. Matchett also suggests an objectives-oriented approach for integration of ethics into college curricula.

22. See the Handbook for Performance Improvement, Pershing, 2006; additional information is available at www.ispi.org. The Pershing text is the 3rd edition of the handbook. While it captures many of the advances in this rapidly evolving and expanding field, there are also many valuable additional resources in the previous two editions (Stolovitch & Keeps, 1992, 1999).

23. Deming, 1972, 1982, 1986; Juran, 1988

24. 1992; citation is from Dean, 1993, p. 11; Trevino, 1987, 1992

25. Watkins, Performance by Design—comment here

26. These elements come from the research base in Human Performance Technology, namely from Stolovich & Keeps, 1999; Villachica & Stone, 1999; Rummler, 2004. This evidence-based model for performance design is also further developed and explained in Wedman & Graham, 1998; Wedman & Diggs, 2001; Watkins, Leigh, & Wedman, in press. This work underscores other references to the main characteristics of a system that must be addressed in order to support effective performance. If we look at ethics in performance terms, then these different aspects are equally as applicable. In designing for desired performance, you'll want to consider how each of these parts of the system support or do not support the desired ethical performance of your organization and individuals within the organization.

27. Bernardez explores the power of entrepreneurial ecosystems to generate a boom or a bust based on the available *social* capital, which is largely determined by national policy and planning. He examines several international case studies and correlational data between national ecosystems and organizational performance in his work "The power of entrepreneurial ecosystems: Extracting 'booms' from 'busts'" (2009).

29. This list refers to recalls of peanuts, potatoes ("Simply Potatoes" products through Giant grocery stores), spinach, baby bottles, toys, and Topps Meat, Inc. that occurred within a one-year period from 2008-2009

30. Personal communications, 2009, spanning the months of May and June; Bernardez has digested some of this into a 2009 article.

Appendix
Ethics by Design: A Detailed Contract for Desired Social Impact

Your Organization's Social Contract

We commit, individually and together, to deliver organizational results that add value for all external clients and society. We recognize that our organization is a part of the larger society, and therefore is an active partner in identifying desirable societal outcomes that result from our services and products. We are committed to getting the facts on the outcomes and tracking our success over time. We choose to design our organization in a manner that clearly accomplishes desired outcomes for external clients and society, desired results for our organization, and desired performance within our organization.

_____

Signed by you, in representation of your organization

Your Contract Deliverables to Society
(Indicators of Societal Impact)

Basic Ideal Vision Elements—There will be no loss of life or elimination of the survival of any species required for human survival. There will be no reductions in levels of self-sufficiency, quality of life, livelihood, or loss of property from any source, including:	My Organization Makes a Contribution...		
	Directly	Indirectly	None
War and/or riot and/or terrorism			
Shelter			

(continued)

Your Contract Deliverables to Society (continued)	My Organization Makes a Contribution...		
	Directly	Indirectly	None
Unintended human-caused changes to the environment, including permanent destruction of the environment and/or rendering it non-renewable.			
Murder, rape, or crimes of violence, robbery, or destruction to property			
Substance abuse			
Disease			
Pollution			
Starvation and/or malnutrition			
Child abuse			
Partner/spouse/elder abuse			
Accidents, including transportation, home, and business/workplace			
Discrimination based on irrelevant variables, including color, race, creed, sex, religion, national origin, age, and location			
Poverty will not exist, and every woman and man will earn at least as much as it costs him or her to live unless he or she is progressing toward being self-sufficient and self-reliant			
No adult will be under the care, custody, or control of another person, agency, or substance. All adult citizens will be self-sufficient and self-reliant as minimally indicated by their consumption being equal to or less than their production			

Evaluating Potential Partners		
Questions Organizations Must Ask about Potential Partners	**Do You Commit:**	
	Yes	No
Does this potential partner commit to deliver products, services, or educational contributions that add value for your externals AND society? (Mega/Outcomes)		
Does this potential partner commit to deliver products, services, or educational contributions that have the quality required by other external partners? (Macro/Outputs)		
Does this potential partner commit to internal results that have the quality required by your internal partners? (Micro/Products)		
Does this potential partner commit to have efficient internal products, programs, projects, and activities? (Processes)		
Does this potential partner commit to create and ensure the quality and appropriateness of the human, capital, and physical resources available? (Inputs)		
Does this potential partner commit to deliver: a. Products, activities, methods, and procedures that have positive value and worth? b. The results and accomplishments defined by our objectives?		
Evaluation/Continuous Improvement		

Our Organization's Strategic Plan
Mega
Macro
Micro
Processes

References

Bernárdez, M. (2005). Achieving Business Success by Developing Clients and Community: Lessons from Leading Companies, Emerging Economies and a Nine Year Case Study. *Performance Improvement Quarterly, 18*(3), 37–55.

Bernardez, M. (2008). Minding the business of business: tools and models to design and measure wealth creation. *PII Review*, 1:1, 12–49.

Bernardez, M. (2009). The power of entrepreneurial ecosystems: extracting boom from bust. *PII Review*, 12–45.

Berenbeim, R. E. (1987). Corporate ethics (Research report #900). New York: The Conference Board.

Brethower, D. (2006). *Performance analysis: Knowing what to do and how.* Amherst, MA., HRD Press.

Chow, A. (2008). *The role of systems design and educational informatics in educational reform: The story of the Central Educational Center.* Unpublished doctoral dissertation, Florida State University.

Chow, A., Whitlock, M. & Moore, S. (2007). *Seamless education: The educational conspiracy across stakeholders in Georgia.* Pi Lambda Theta Leadership Conference (July 2007).

Davis, I. (2005). The biggest contract. *The Economist,* 28 May 2005, 69–71.

Davis, M. (1999). *Ethics and the university.* London: Routledge.

Dean, P.J. (1993). A selected review of the underpinnings of ethics for human performance technology professionals—Part One: Key ethical theories and research. *Performance Improvement Quarterly, 6*(4), 3–32.

Delaney, J. & Sockell, D. (1992). Do company ethics training programs make a difference? An empirical analysis. *Journal of Business Ethics, 11*, 719–727.

Deming, W. E. (1972). Code of professional conduct. *International Statistics Review, 40*(2), 215–219.

Deming, W. E. (1982). *Quality, productivity, and competitive position.* Cambridge: MIT, Center for Advanced Engineering Study.

Deming, W. E. (1986). *Out of the crisis.* Cambridge: MIT, Center for Advanced Engineering Technology.

Dobni, D., Ritchie, J.R., & Zerbe, W. (2000). Organizational values: The inside view of service productivity. *Journal of Business Research, 47*, 91–107.

Drucker, P. (1984). *The temptation to do good.* New York: Harper & Row.

Drucker, P.F. (1985). *Innovation and entrepreneurship: Practices and principles.* New York: Harper & Row.

Drucker, P.F. (1989). *The new realities: In government and politics/in economics and business/in society and world view.* New York: Harper & Row.

Drucker, P. F. (1995). *Managing in a time of great change.* New York: Truman Talley Books/Dutton.

Ellsworth, J. (2009). Personal communication received May 15, 2009.

Estes, R. (1996). *Tyranny of the bottom line: Why corporations make good people do bad things.* San Francisco: Berrett-Koehler. Lee, M. (2003). On codes of ethics, the individual and performance. *Performance Improvement Quarterly, 16*(2), 72–89.

Frankel, M. (1989). Professional codes: Why, how, and with what impact? *Journal of Business Ethics, 8*, 109–115.

Gladwell, M. (2008). *Outliers: The story of successes.* New York: Little Brown and Company.

Grajew, O. (2007). Beyond corporate social responsibility. Podcast from Stanford University as part of the Social Entrepreneurship series. July 15, 2007. Available on iTunes.

Grzywacz, J. G., Carlson, D. S., Kacmar, K. M., & Wayne, J. H. (2007). Work-family facilitation: A multilevel perspective on the synergies between work and family. *Journal of Occupational and Organizational Psychology, 80,* 559–574.

Grzywacz, J. G., Casey, P. R., & Jones, F. A. (2007). Workplace flexibility and employee health behaviors: A cross-sectional and longitudinal analysis. *Journal of Occupational and Environmental Medicine, 49,* 1302-1309.

Guerra, I. & Rodriguez, G. (2005). Educational planning and social responsibility: Eleven years of Mega planning at the Sonora Institute of Technology (ITSON). *Performance Improvement Quarterly, 18*(3), 56–64.

Hammond, 1992 is cited in Dean, P.J. (1993). A selected review of the underpinnings of ethics for human performance technology professionals—Part One: Key ethical theories and research. *Performance Improvement Quarterly, 6*(4), 3–32.

Harrington, S. J. (1991). What corporate America is teaching about ethics. *The Executive, 5,* 1–12.

Hatcher, T. (2002). *Ethics and HRD: A new approach to leading responsible organizations.* Cambridge, MA: Perseus.

Hatcher, T. (2003). Social responsibility as an ethical imperative in performance improvement. *Performance Improvement Quarterly, 16*(2), 105–121.

Hobbes, Thomas. *Leviathan* (1651)

HR Focus, (2005). How HR can facilitate ethics. *HR Focus, 82*(4), 11–12.

Juran, J. M. (1988). *Juran on planning for quality.* New York: Free Press.

Kaufman, R. (1972). *Educational system planning.* Englewood Cliffs, NJ: Prentice Hall.

Kaufman, R. (1997). A new reality for organizational success: Two bottom lines. *Performance Improvement, 38*(8), 3.

Kaufman, R. (2000). *Mega planning: Practical tools for organizational success.* Thousand Oaks, CA: Sage Publications.

Kaufman, R. (2006a). *Change, choices, and consequences: A guide to mega thinking and planning.* Amherst, MA: HRD Press.

Kaufman, R. (2006b). *30 seconds that can change your life: A decision-making guide for those who refuse to be mediocre.* Amherst, MA. HRD Press Inc.

Kaufman, R., Corrigan, R., & Johnson, D. (1969). Towards educational responsiveness to society's needs: A tentative utility model. *Socio-Economic Planning Sciences, 3,* 151–157.

Kaufman, R, & Guerra-Lopez, I. (2008) *The assessment book: applied strategic thinking and performance improvement through self-assessments.* Amherst, MA. HRD Press Inc.

Kaufman, R. & Lick, D. (2000). *Performance in* Practice—an ASTD Newsletter: Winter 2000-2001; pp 8–9.

Kaufman, R., Oakley-Browne, H., Watkins, R., & Leigh, D. (2003). System (and systems) thinking. In Ed. R. Kaufman, *Strategic planning for success: Aligning people, performance, and payoffs.* San Francisco: Jossey-Bass/Pfeiffer.

Kaufman, R. & Watkins, R. (1999) Using an ideal vision to guide Florida's revision of the State Comprehensive Plan: A sensible approach to add value for citizens. In DeHaven-Smith, L. (Ed.) *Florida's future: A guide to revising Florida's State Comprehensive Plan.* Tallahassee, FL: Florida Institute of Government.

Lee, M. (2003). On codes of ethics, the individual and performance. *Performance Improvement Quarterly, 16*(2), 72–89.

Lick, D. W. & Kaufman, R. (2000). Change creation: The rest of the planning story. Chapter 2 in *Technology-driven change: Principles to practice.* Ann Arbor, MI: Society for College and University Planning.

Locke, J. (1690). *Second treatise on government.*

Mager, R. F. (1997). *Preparing instructional objectives: A critical tool in the development of effective instruction* (3rd ed.). Atlanta, GA: CEP Press.

Mager, R. F. & Pipe, P. (1997). *Analyzing performance problems, or you really oughta wanna: How to figure out why people aren't doing what they should be, and what to do about it* (3rd ed.). Atlanta, GA: CEP Press.

Mager, R. F. (1997). *Preparing instructional objectives.* Atlanta, GA: Center for Effective Performance.

Martinez, M.N. (1998). An inside look at making the grade. *HR Magazine*, March 1998.

McClelland, D. (1961). *The achieving society.* Princeton, NJ: D. Van Nostrand.

McDonough, W. (2006). Cradle to cradle design. iTunesU— Stanford series. Dec. 3, 2006. Accessed Jan. 15, 2008.

McNerney, D.J. (1996). Employee motivation: Creating a motivated workforce. *HRFocus*, August 1996.

Moore, S. L. (2005). *The social responsibility of a profession: An analysis of factors influencing ethics and the teaching of social responsibility in educational technology programs.* Unpublished doctoral dissertation. Greeley, CO: University of Northern Colorado.

Moore, S.L., Ellsworth, J., and Kaufman, R. (2008). Objectives: Are they useful? A Quick Assessment. *Performance Improvement, 47*(7), 41–47.

National Education Association. "Code of Ethics of the Education Profession," 1975. Retrieved Oct. 24, 2008, http://www.nea.org/aboutnea/code.html.

Pava, M.L. & Krausz, J. (1995). *Corporate social responsibility and financial performance.* Westport, CT: Greenwood Publishers.

Pershing, J.A. (2006). *Handbook of human performance technology: Principles practices potential.* San Francisco: Pfeiffer.

Peters, T. & Waterman, R. (1982). *In search of excellence.* New York: Harper and Row.

Petrick, J. & Scherer, R. (2003). The Enron scandal and neglect of management integrity capacity. *Mid-America Journal of Business, 18*(1), 37–49.

Popcorn, F. (1991). *The popcorn report.* New York: Doubleday.

Porter, M., & Kramer, M.R. (2002). The competitive advantage of corporate philanthropy. *Harvard Business Review,* December, 56–58.

Porter, M. & Kramer, M. (2006). Strategy & society: The link between competitive advantage and corporate social responsibility. *Harvard Business Review, 84*(12), 78–92.

Prahalad, C.K., & Hammond, A. (2002). Serving the world's poor, profitably. *Harvard Business Review, 80*(9), 48–57.

Rogers, E. (2003). *Diffusion of innovations* (5th ed). New York: Free Press.

Rousseau, Jean-Jacques. *The social contract, or principles of political right* (1762).

Sample, J. (2007). *Avoiding legal liability for adult educators, human resource developers, and instructional designers.* Malabar, FL: Krieger Publishing Co.

Siegel, P., Mosca, J., & Karim, K. (1997). Impact of flexible work hours on organizational commitment and job satisfaction in small business organizations. *Journal of Business and Entrepreneurship,* 81–98.

Spector, P. (2006). *Industrial organizational psychology* (4th ed). Upper Saddle River, NJ: Prentice Hall.

Stolovitch, H., & Keeps, E. (Eds.). (1992). *Handbook of human performance technology* (1st ed.). San Francisco: Jossey-Bass.

Stolovitch, H., & Keeps, E. (Eds.). (1999). *Handbook of human performance technology* (2nd ed.). San Francisco: Jossey-Bass.

Trevino, L. (1987). *The influences of vicarious learning and individual differences on ethical decision making in the organization: An experiment.* Unpublished doctoral dissertation. Texas A&M University.

Trevino, L. (1992). Moral reasoning and business ethics: Implications for research, education, and management. *Journal of Business Ethics, 11,* 445–459.

Verschoor, C. (1998). Corporations' financial performance and its commitment to ethics. *Journal of Business Ethics, 17,* 1509–1516.

Volcker, P., Norris, F., & Bockelman, C. (2000). The New York Times century of business. New York: McGraw-Hill.

von Bertalanffy, L. (1951). General system theory - A new approach to unity of science (symposium), *Human Biology, 23,* 303–361.

von Bertalanffy, L. (1969). *General system theory: Foundations, development, applications (revised edition).* New York: George Braziller.

Watkins, R. (2007). *Performance by design: The systematic selection, design, development of performance technologies that produce useful results.* Amherst, MA: HRD Press.

Weaver, G. R. (1999). Compliance and values oriented ethics programs: Influences on employee's attitudes and behavior. *Business Ethics Quarterly, 9,* 315–335.

Weiss, N. (1998). How Starbucks impassions workers to drive growth. *Workforce,* August 1998.

About the Author

Stephanie L. Moore, Ph.D. is Lecturer and Director of Engineering Instructional Design at the University of Virginia in the School of Engineering and Applied Science where she teaches Business Ethics for Engineers. Her primary project is the delivery of the distance undergraduate engineering program, engineers **produced** in Virginia. This program focuses on delivering the opportunity for traditionally underrepresented populations to complete a bachelor's in engineering without leaving their communities. The team's work has a particular focus on workforce development and individual and community self-sufficiency. Stephanie is the chief architect of this program's evaluation plan, which includes the components of social responsibility discussed in this book.

Additionally, she collaborates with the Curry School of Engineering on children's engineering and digital fabrication initiatives. Prior to joining UVA, she worked at the University of Northern Colorado, first as Lead Instructional Designer for the National Center on Low-Incidence Disabilities designing fully accessible online environments for users with a range of disabilities, garnering the 2001 AACTE Innovation of the Year Award. She then worked for the Office of Institutional Assessment on national accreditation and program evaluation. She has also worked for the Colorado Department of Education as Assessment Coordinator focused on K-3 literacy instruction and assessment.

Stephanie's primary research and publication interests are strategic planning and accountability, assessment and evaluation, system ethics, ethics of technology, professional ethics, and distributed learning systems, including a recent guest edited volume of *New Directions for Higher Education: Practical Approaches to Ethics for Colleges and Universities*.